Rumours of

soft
fantasy shapes

juicy succulence

dancing

in lace

half in shadows
half in light

all in elemental bliss ....

Other books by Julia Trops

2011 Okanagan Erotic Art Show Catalog
Simplicity in Mind - catalog for the Livessence Society for Figurative Artists and Models
2009 Okanagan Erotic Art Show Catalog
Lauren - Sensuality of Form
Donnalee (forthcoming)

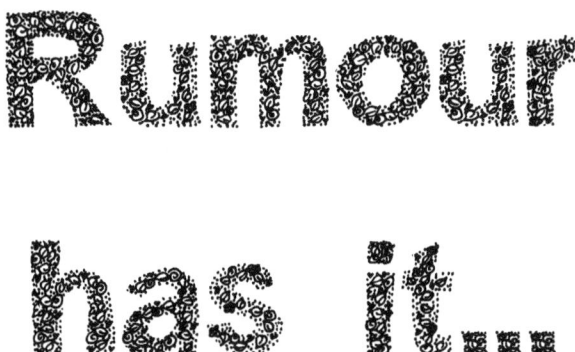

Rumour has it...

2012 Okanagan Erotic Art Show Catalog

Ex Nihilo Vineyards

24 May to 22 June 2012
http://www.okanaganeroticartshow.com

Published by Julia Trops ISBN 978-0-9813363-3-6

Cover artwork used with permission by Kai Eckhardt, titled The Frame
Photograph of Gary Mitchell by Michelle Waters, all rights reserved.
Photograph of Ex Nihilo Vineyards by Susan Whitney and Larry MacDougall

Font: title page: Janda Rosalie
Paragraphs: Adobe Garamond Pro

Preface

The Okanagan Erotic Show emerged in 2007, fellow artists Lauren Wilson, Angela Hansen and myself were talking about having an art show that was a bit more exciting than the usual run of the mill life drawing exhibitions. We were having a glass (or two, maybe more, I can't remember) of wine while manning the Livessence booth at one of the local art shows, and noticed there were many people who would barely glance at the nudes on display. Censorship about what was "proper" had reared its ugly head once again. Knowing full well that erotic is perceived individually, we wanted to shake things up. We wanted to have some FUN!

The first show, "Blush, what makes you?" at the Rotary Centre for the Arts (RCA) in 2008 was a huge success, but as you can imagine, as the RCA is a public building, there were a few complaints. The interest, though, was definitely there. In 2009, Angela went on to have her first child, and Lauren went traveling in Asia, so that year, I carried on my own, and have since. "Raw...Whispers" was at A. Woodside Design Gallery, and that year I created the first catalog. I realized how important that record seemed to be to each artist.

2010 saw a bit of rough bumps and grinds, but that experience showed me where we, the Okanagan artists, were in terms of comfort level and where we, the public, were in terms of artistic support and adventure. Finally, "Seduce Me" was held at Ex Nihilo Vineyards. I was overwhelmed by the attendance at the opening night, and the tremendously positive comments on the show throughout its run, by both artists and attendees. 2011's Edge of Night was overwhelming with around 300 attendees at opening night, many of the artists, and patrons who dressed up! 2012 is a ticketed Opening Night with a third of the proceeds going to the chosen charity.

Opening the Call to the United States in 2010 onward was the right thing to do. There is no catalog for 2010, as it was all timing or rather lack of time, due to the circumstances experienced, but there is a catalog for 2011 and hopefully there will be one for each year going forward.

In 2011 and again in 2012, I am thrilled to see one of the original creators of the show, Angela Hansen, come back as an artist participant. Welcome back!

Introduction

An artist's expression is a search for self identity, and a statement of their place in the world, or what they perceive to be their place in the world. It is communication whereby we, as artists, provide a dialog for interaction between ourselves and those who engage with the work, regardless if they like it or not, or understand it or not.

Is all art erotic? I believe that yes it is, in that all art is playfully engaging the mind, the emotions, and maybe even the physical senses. Art is sensual in all aspects of the word. All art is suggestive and vulnerable by its request for your participation. Art is created from desire, a desire to explore, to discover, to understand, and to be understood.

But what makes something erotic?

Eroticism is only perceived through emotion and imagination. The mystical, the uncanny, the provocative, the forbidden, the hidden. There are varying levels of what one can consider as erotic, each as flexible as individual boundaries allow. The erotic can be fun and playful, it can be sexy, it can be thoughtful, it can be intelligent. For some, erotic can be nonsense, it can be elusive, evocative, mysterious, and metaphoric. For others, it can be descriptive, illustrative, explicit. It is always a mirror reflecting our vulnerability.

The erotic can be all of this, experienced on the journey from one's self, our journey on the way to *la petite mort*: the giving up of one's identity in order to facilitate a spiritual union with the divine.

Many works in this show, and many of the other Erotic Art Shows I have seen, have a great deal of work relating to the female form. As an artist, I ask myself is that an easy out? Is it such a cliche that simply by having a female, the artist has 90% of the work done for them? And on the other hand, I think some people think that any work containing a female nude is erotic, simply by her presence. Maybe both theories are right.

Many believe the female form is symbolic of the highest form of sensual expression. Through imagination, it can be manifested, for example, in landscapes, and food. The feminine brand suggests to us the mysteries of life and the universe; it suggests rumours of the unknown. In human understanding, the female body is representative of all sacred space: from the juncture of tree limbs, to groves in a forest, to the rolling hills, to the hidden spaces within fruit and foods where seeds are kept, to man-made places where one "worships" or "creates".

The feminine and aspects of the female form, represent our interpretation and evocation of the universe, and that mysterious, life-giving energy to which we long to unite, and embrace, and succumb. For the male artist and viewer, it is an offering to request entry in to that divine space, but for the female it is to self-actualize, for she is already there.

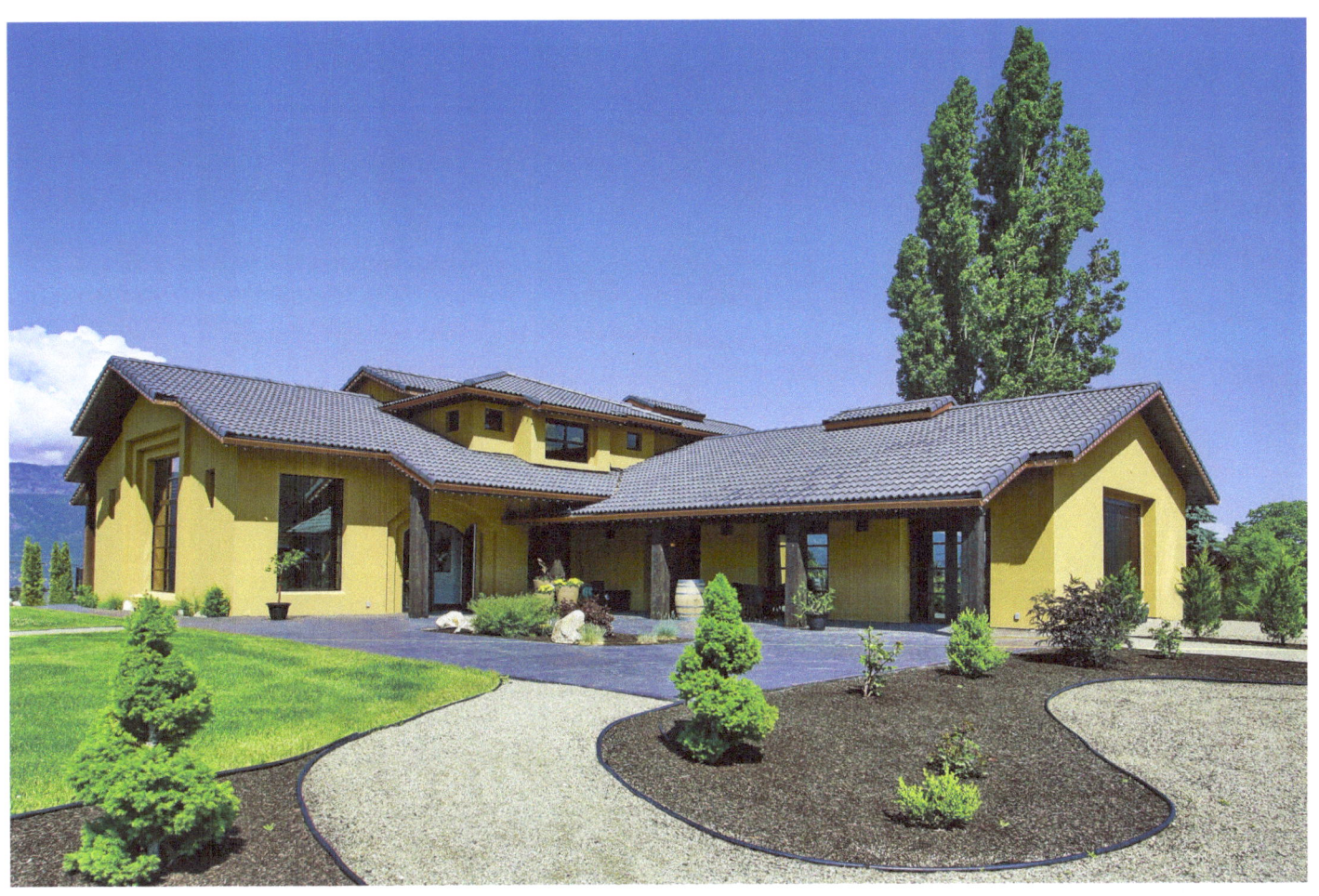

Ex Nihilo Vineyards
1525 Camp Road
Lake Country, BC

http://www.exnihilovineyards.com

Proprietors:
Jeff and Decoa Harder, Jay and Twila Paulson

The Artists

Aarron Laidig
AJ Jaeger
Amy Burkard
Angela Bonten
Angela Hansen
Avocado Salad
Brenda Maunders
Brittany Falk
Chris Goncalves
Christine Allan
Corey Mazurat
Craig Warner
Dan Irvine
Dan McCormack
Dongmin Lai
Ellen Houben
Gail Marie Kern
Gary Mitchell
Gerry Greengrove
Gracie Ackerman
Jackie Champion

Jaime Seward
Jaine Buse
James Postill
Jeffrey Bain
Jennifer Burrows
Jessica Klein
Jessika Von Innerebner
Jim Britton
Joyce Krenn
Julia Trops
June Seed
Kai Eckhardt
Karla Warkotsch
Kendi Clearwater
Kimberly Walker
Lisolette Gilcrest
Logan Miller
Lynn Erin
Margot Stolz
Marianne Dashwood
Mario Vucinovic

Martha Moore
Mary Anne Domarchuk
Michelle Stephenson
Neal Campbell
Patricia Gulyas
Paul Butvila
Randal Sweet
Rena Warren
River Lewis
Robert Verigin
Robin McDonald
Roxi Sim Hermsen
Ryan Robson
Sandra Windsor
Sea Dean
Shannon Breadner
Sharr
Suzanne LeStage
Teri Blackwell
Tina Aziz-Siddiqui
Wendy Pros

Aarron Laidig

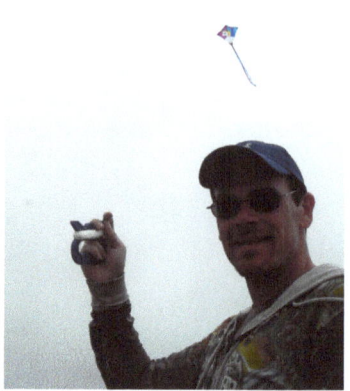

Aarron Laidig was born in 1969 in a small Pacific Northwest logging town and raised by a hippie era, artist father. His peculiar habit of stopping everything to make an artistic vision become reality made a day job something not possible, but luck or fate smiled upon him and he found to his delight that enough people enjoyed his artistic visions that he would need do nothing else in life except make the pictures in his mind a reality to support himself on the crazy planet called earth.

http://www.twitter.com/RedRegion

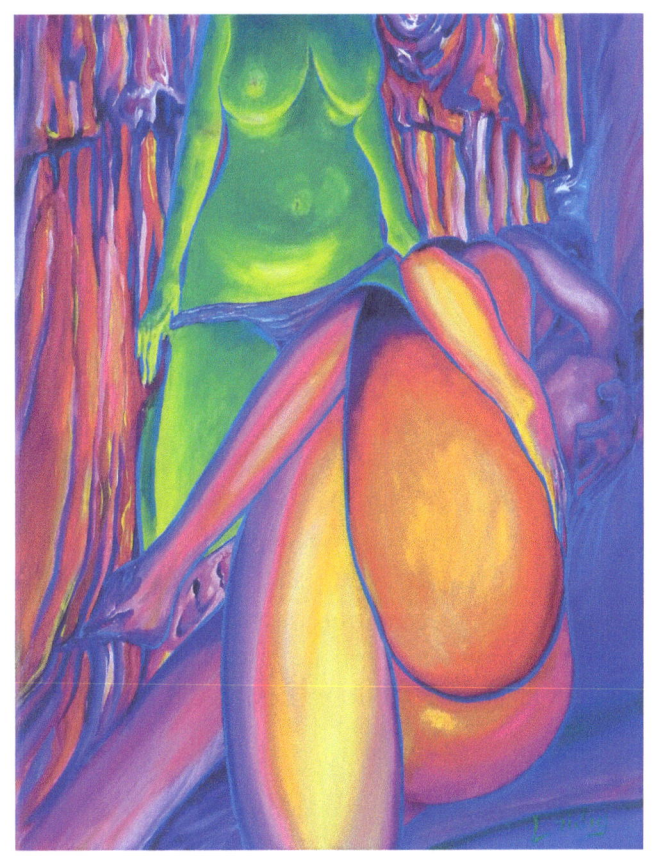

It's Happening
Aarron Laidig
16" x 12"
Acrylic on Canvas

Always stirring the pot of life with lust.

AJ Jaeger

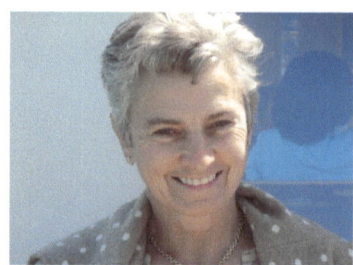

aj (initials for angelika jaeger) hails from Germany. The family settled in the Okanagan Valley, British Columbia, where aj began exploring the world of creating artwork. aj is active in the art world. She conducts regular workshops in mixed media and collage as well she has organized numerous art exhibitions throughout the Okanagan. As part of her commitment to her community, aj has served for several years as the President of the Vernon Public Art Gallery and as Chairperson for the North Okanagan Chapter of Federation of Canadian Artists. She is part of the Kelowna Artists Collective 'Ars Longa', now in its 10th year.

http://www.angelikajaeger.com

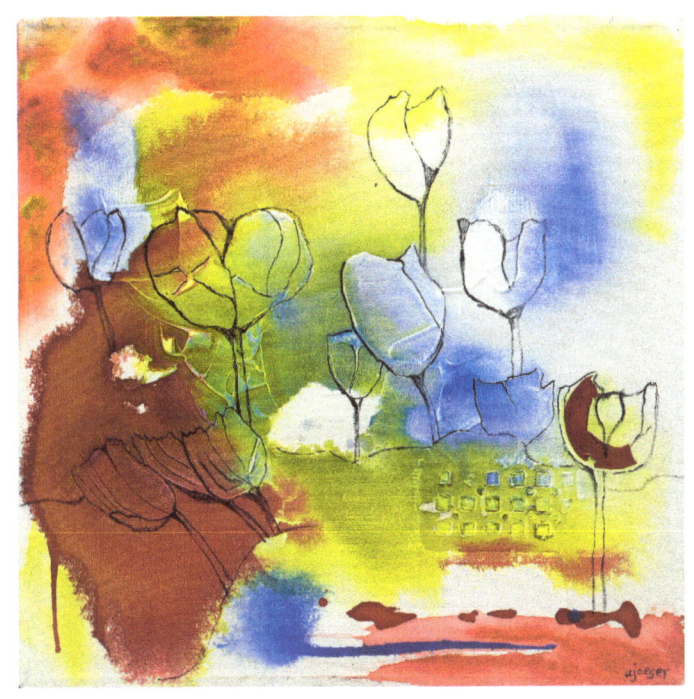

Power Color
AJ Jaeger
24" x 24"
Mixed Media

Colors create their own Power.

Amy Burkard

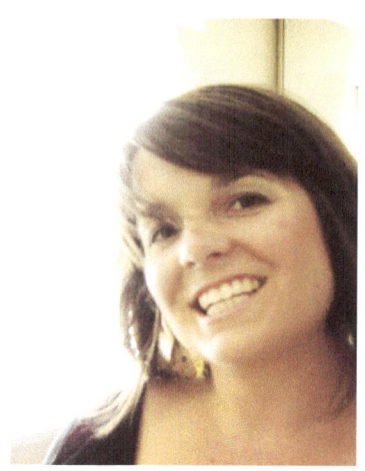

Amy Burkard is a Kelowna-based visual artist who has been presenting work professionally for over 10 years. In her early 20's she travelled Europe, this experience enhanced her outlook on life. Shortly thereafter she completed her BFA at Emily Carr and her creative voice as female artist emerged. She remains determined and curious. Amy now spends her days as a full time artist and teacher. Her "artistic borders are open", allowing room for experimentation and creative growth.

http://www.amybydesign.ca

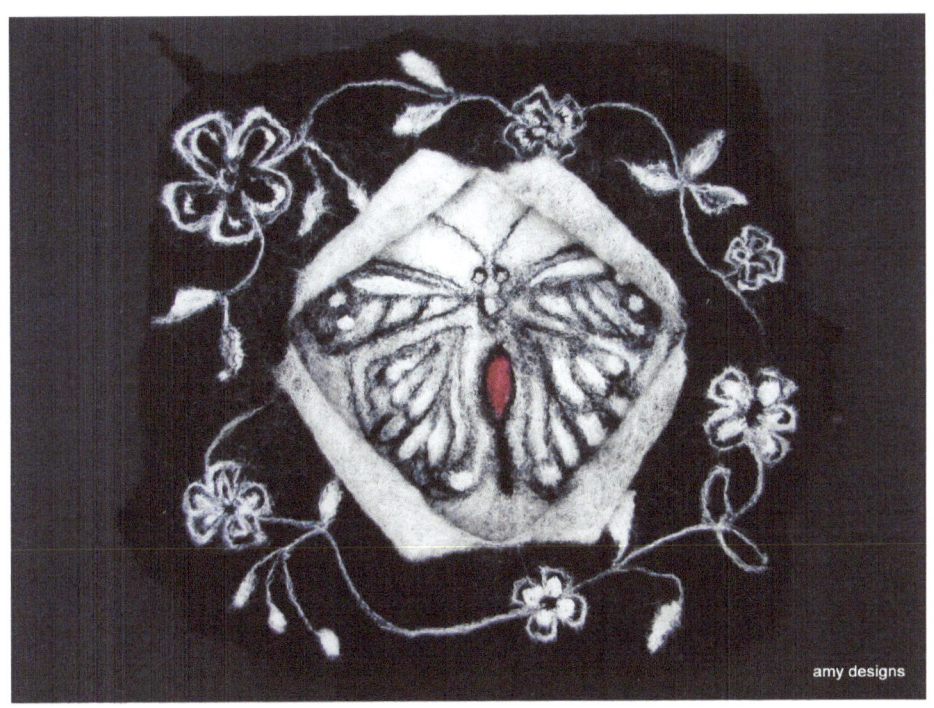

amy designs

Emergence
Amy Burkard
12" x 12"
Alpaca, Wool, & Silk

I take pleasure in working with tactile and sensual materials, with a vision for my final work I reinvent meaning through revealing visual imagery.

Angela Bonten

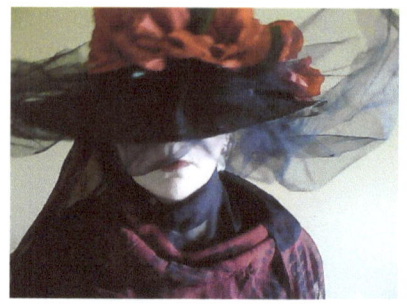

Angela Bonten is a graduate of Grant MacEwan University College, Edmonton, fibre and fine art programs and arts administration program. Her gypsy soul has taken her on many travel adventures, from her native Wales to Newfoundland, and also Nova Scotia, where she owned a bead shop for many years and becoming a jewellery designer and instructor. She presently resides in B.C. and is a resident artist at the Rotary Centre for the Arts, Kelowna. Her energetic, flamboyant persona is reflected in her art, but also, like her paintings, beneath the surface, there is a mystery of secrets and desires to be discovered.

http://www.angelabonten.com

Historical reference:
"In 1748 "Memoirs of a Woman of Pleasure" also know as "Fanny Hill" was published. It was considered to be the first pornographic book. The author John Clealand was arrested and charged with "corruption of the kings subjects"

It was not until 1960 that an unexpurgated copy of "Fanny Hill" was published. Subsequently a charge of obscenity was issued against the publisher. The defence argued that Fanny Hill was a historical source book and that it was a joyful celebration of normal non-perverted sex—bawdy rather than pornographic. It wasn't until 1970 that the book was republished.

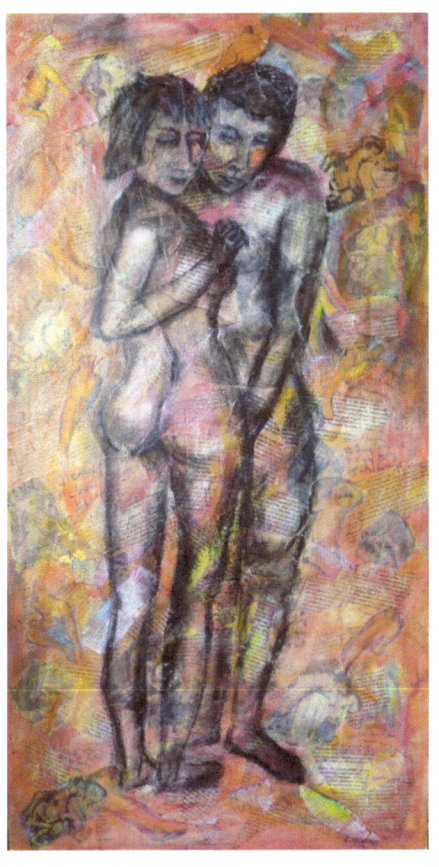

Fanny, you've cum a long way ....
Angela Bonten
48" x 24"
Mixed Media

This art piece juxtaposes the writings and images of the book with contemporary sexual internet letters and personal thoughts. I am exploring the issues of freedom of sexuality and questioning the boundaries of my own sexuality.

Angela Hansen

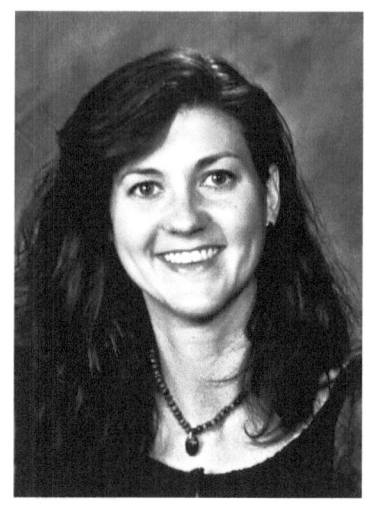

I grew up in the small BC interior town of Quesnel and moved to Vancouver directly after high school to attend the Emily Carr Institute of Art and Design where I received a Bachelor of Design. I worked for quite a few years as a graphic designer then returned to post-secondary to earn my high-school teaching degree from UVic. I have been an art teacher in SD23 for over eleven years now, and am currently teaching art and media arts at George Elliot Secondary in Lake Country. I have been married for almost 9 years and have a gorgeous 3-year old son.

http://www.angelahansenart.com

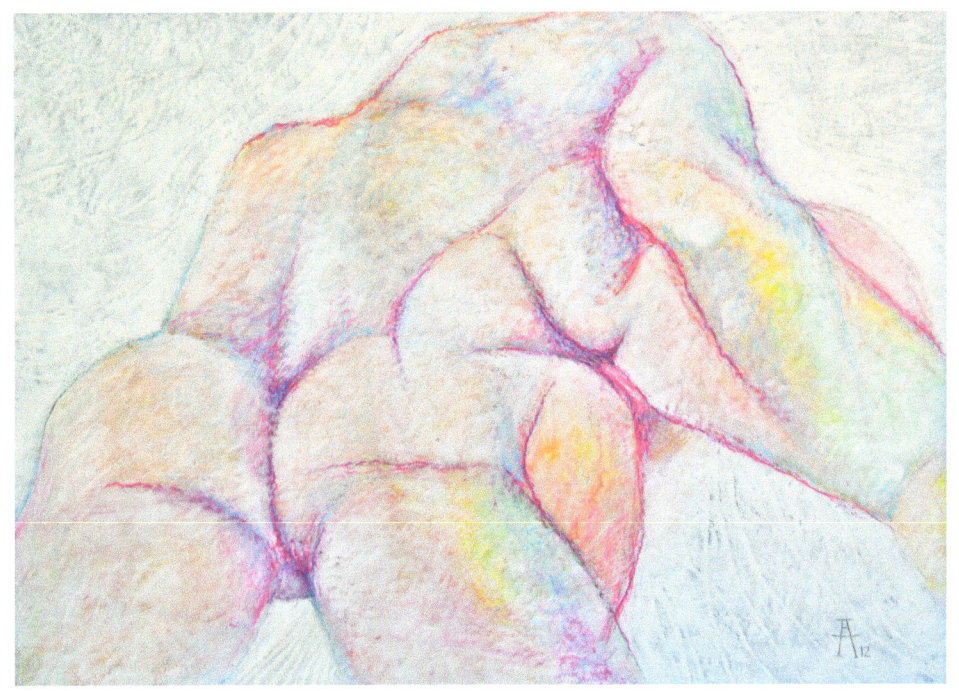

WonderfulElectricMemory
Angela Hansen
18" x 24"
Encaustic

Like a fading dream, the memory of a caress, a kiss, a whisper, skin on skin;
synapses firing... electrical tension.

Avocado Salad

Avocado Salad is a pseudonym of a well known Okanagan artist.

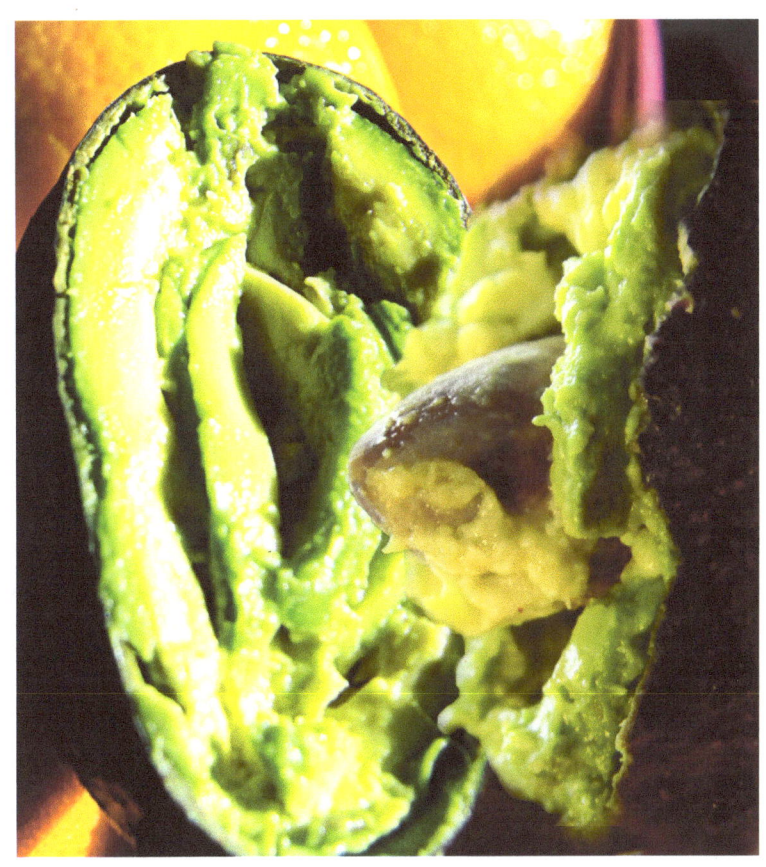

Avocado Salad
11" x 14"
Digital Manipulation

The mysteries and secrets of probing satisfaction.

Brenda Maunders

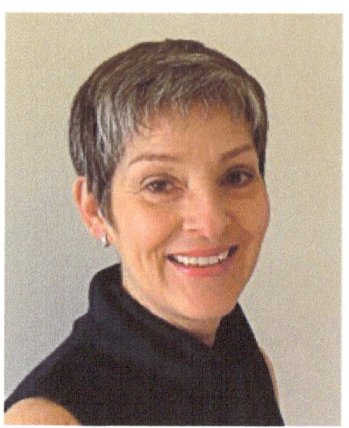

Rich, young, talented, and gorgeous, with legs up to here. Well, not quite - hope springs eternal. Perhaps a more accurate description would be happy, healthy, early-retired, and newly established in lovely Peachland, BC with my wonderful husband Barry. Painting and sculpture are a passion (along with Barry). I've been at this second career long enough to have my art in a few private and corporate collections - but not long enough to have my own show. Some day...

http://artisanatwork.mosaicglobe.com

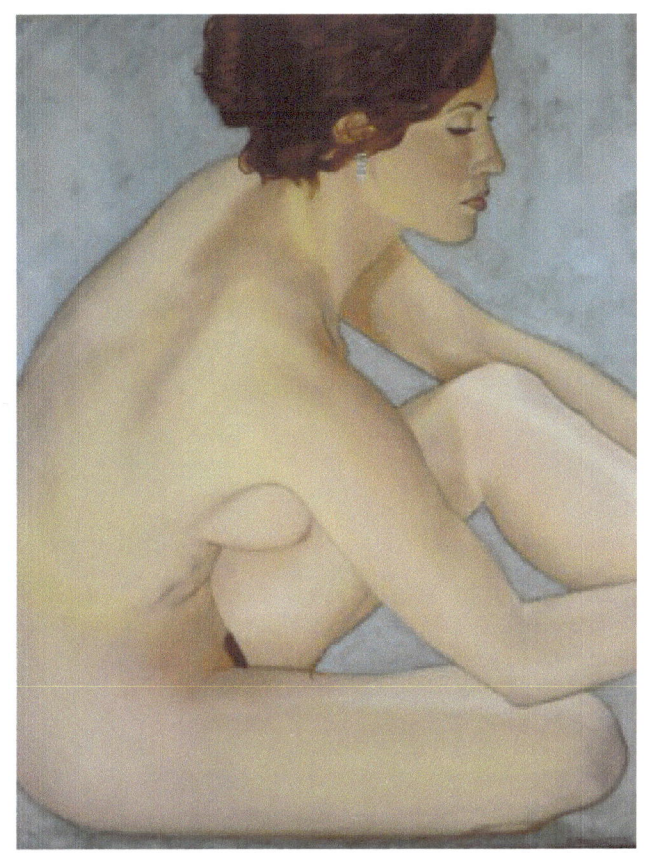

I wonder if I'm overdressed
Brenda Maunders
24" x 18"
Oil on Canvas

Contemplating the night to come.

Brittany Falk

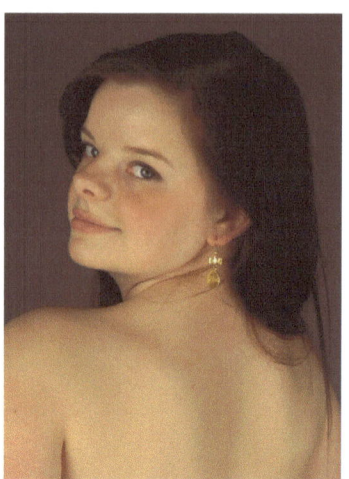

I recently completed my Bachelors of Fine Arts at the University of British Columbia this June. I have been involved in organizing Prevalent Material and Art on the Line, two other prominent local events. I hope to continue to contribute to our art community.

Participating in this event last year broadened my interest into less classical renditions of the nude. While I have always loved the human form, I recently became captivated by the changes that appear when we fall into sleep.

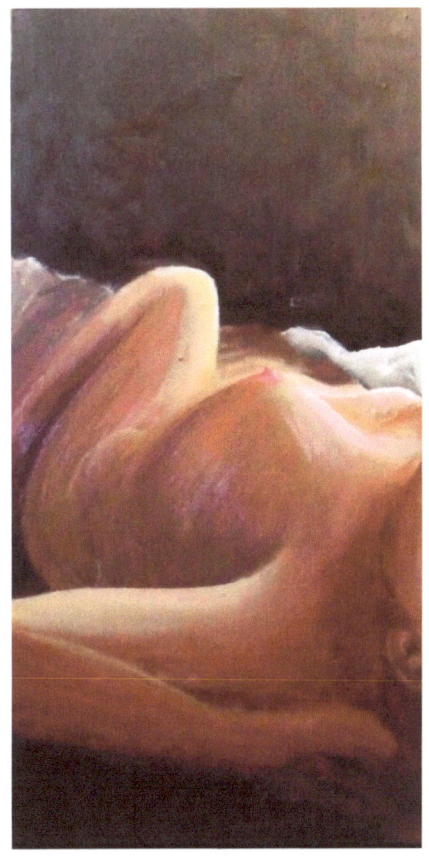

Afternoon Rest
Brittany Falk
24" x 12"
Oil on Canvas

Come join me.

Chris Goncalves

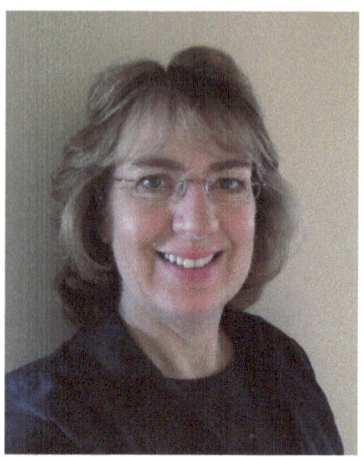

Chris Goncalves has been Woodcarving for 28 years. She immigrated to Ontario, Canada from England in the mid 70's and was very involved in the Woodcarving community there. In 1996 she relocated with her family to Kelowna BC where she now works in the Art and Picture Framing industry and continues to teach, conduct lectures and workshops, and Carve as much as possible. Chris is skilled in many aspects of Carving and Scroll Saw Art. She has won awards and ribbons at many shows over the years and has sold her work internationally.

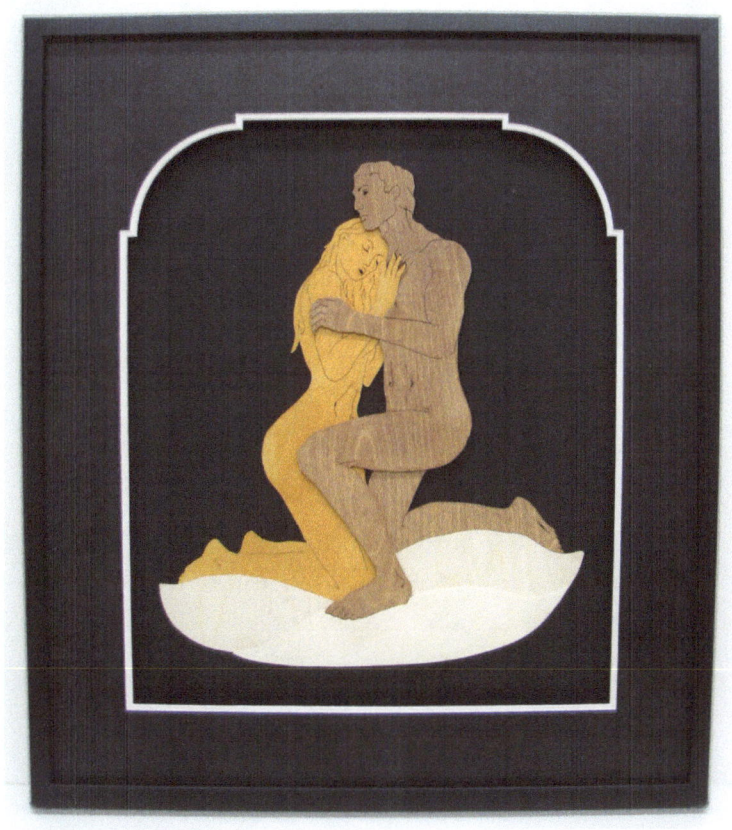

Pillow Talk
Chris Goncalves
32" x 28"
Baltic Birch, Wood – Scroll Saw Art

This piece represents Pure, Uninhibited, Naked Truth & Honesty between Man & Woman.

Christine Allan

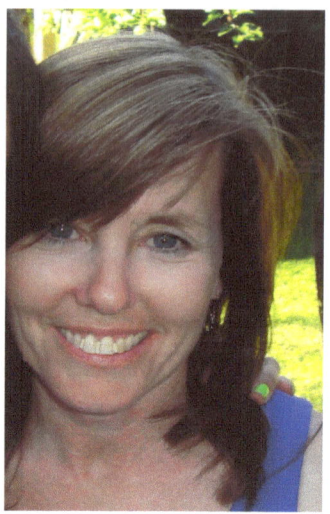

Christine Allan, lives in Chemainus, with her husband and two daughters. She is a mostly self-taught artist who has been creating art in one way or another for most of her life. Art is a passion as well as a refuge for her. Christine creates art from photographs she takes of people, her travels, and her love of the Cowichan Valley and everything in it. She does commissions and regularly donates pieces to raise funds for Cancer research and other charities.

http://www.chrisallanartgallery.com

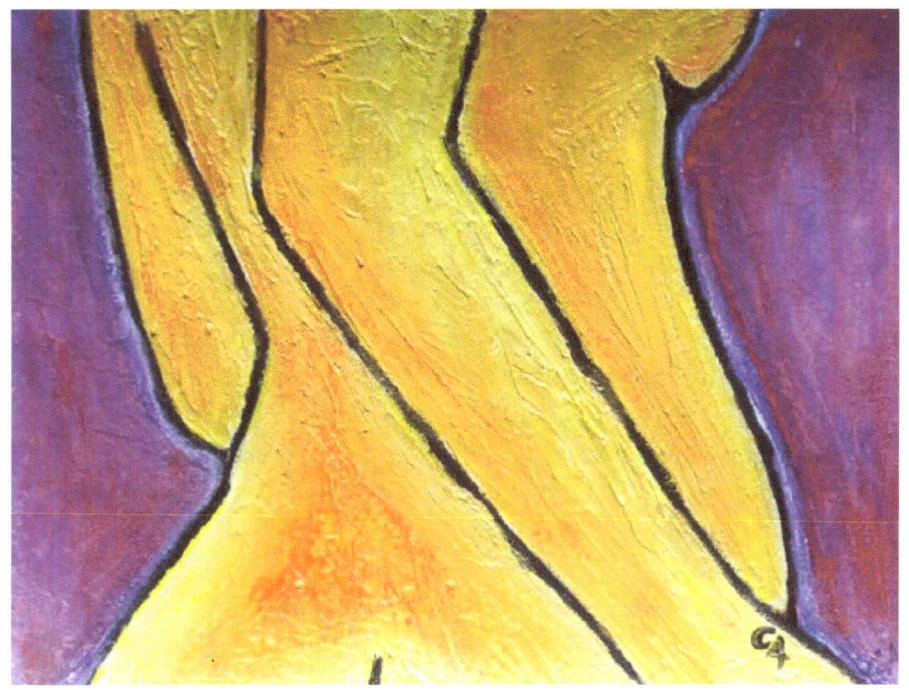

Back
Christine Allan
17" x 14"
Mixed media on watercolour paper

The curves of a womans body attract me to paint them in vibrant colours.

Corey Mazurat

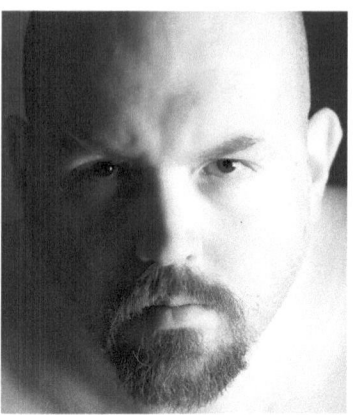

Corey Mazurat has been a photographer for over 25 years. He has shot on three continents and his work has been published across Canada and around the world. He is slightly obsessed with locks, skulls, creepy stuff, horror movies, dangerous sharp objects, and (despite being a life-long atheist) occult things. He dislikes idle chit-chat, social gatherings, mini-vans, children and animal products of any form. He's also rather partial to the colour black.

Founder of www.skurostudios.com, Corey is always willing to entertain the possibility of new and unusual photo shoots, especially when they include rope.

He's happily married to a normal woman.

http://www.skurostudios.com

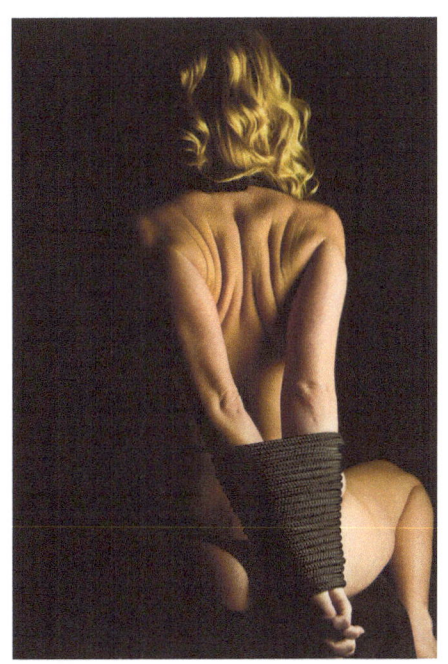

Tied Up
Corey Mazurat
19" x 13"
Inkjet Colour Photographic Print

Everyone needs a little discipline now and then.

Craig Warner

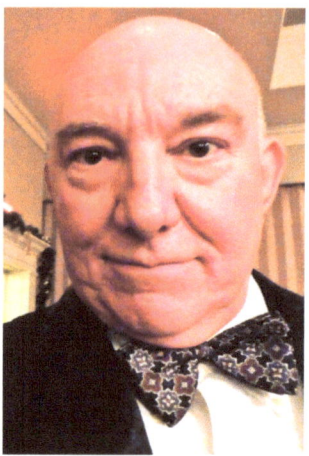

Craig Warner was born in Freeport, NY in 1950. A graduate of the Nova Scotia College of Art and Design, he worked in NYC as a graphic designer from 1979 to 2003. In 2003 he relocated with his wife to her hometown of Vernon, BC. He is an avid golfer and photographer.

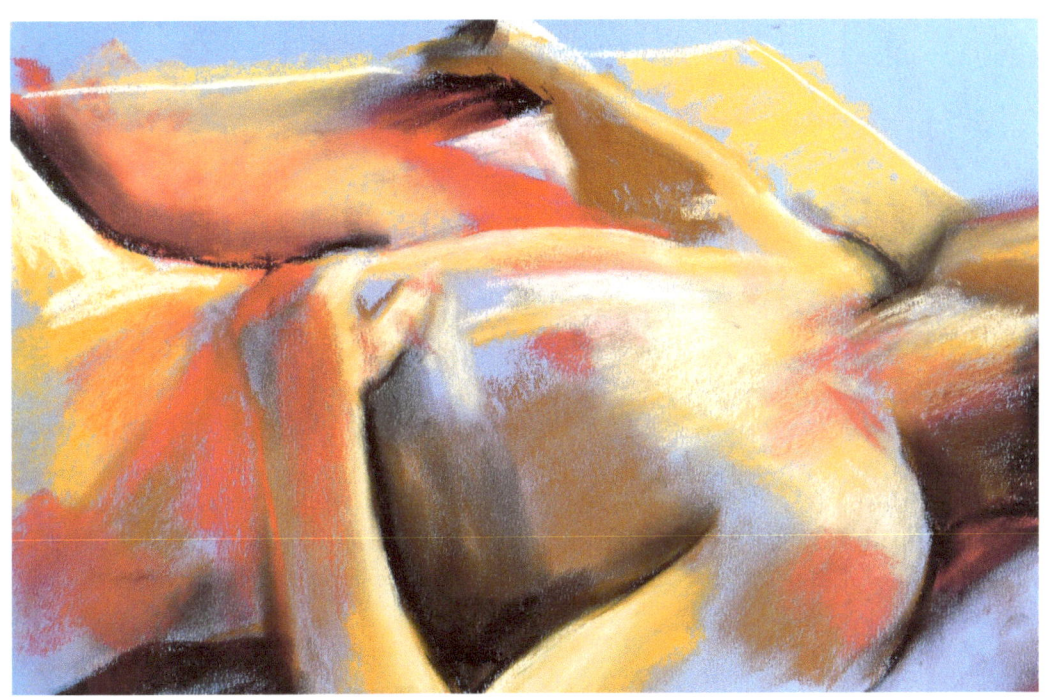

Reclining Male
Craig Warner
19.5" x 25.5"
Pastel on Paper

As a rule I prefer female models, but this drawing caused me to reconsider my inclination.

Dan Irvine

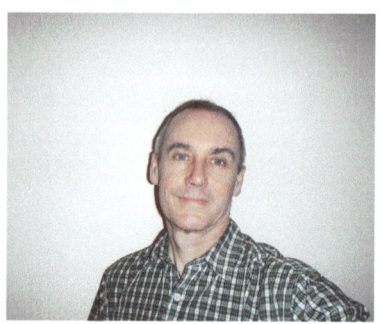

Originally from Vancouver Island I moved to the NWT at 18 years of age. Living inYellowknife and working in many locations across the arctic for 13 years reinforced my inherent tendency to gravitate towards natural environments. Moving to the Okanagan in 1986 allowed this passion to broaden and deepen. Intuitively knowing that time spent in the outdoor beauty surrounding me plays an intrinsic role in feeling whole, I feel lucky to enjoy ski touring and sailing as part of this process. My artistic process flows best when a healthy balance of this lifestyle and studio time are maintained. Re-arranging my life around Stonegarden Studio in 2011 is allowing me to focus more on my creative nature and increasingly see the world through an artists eye.

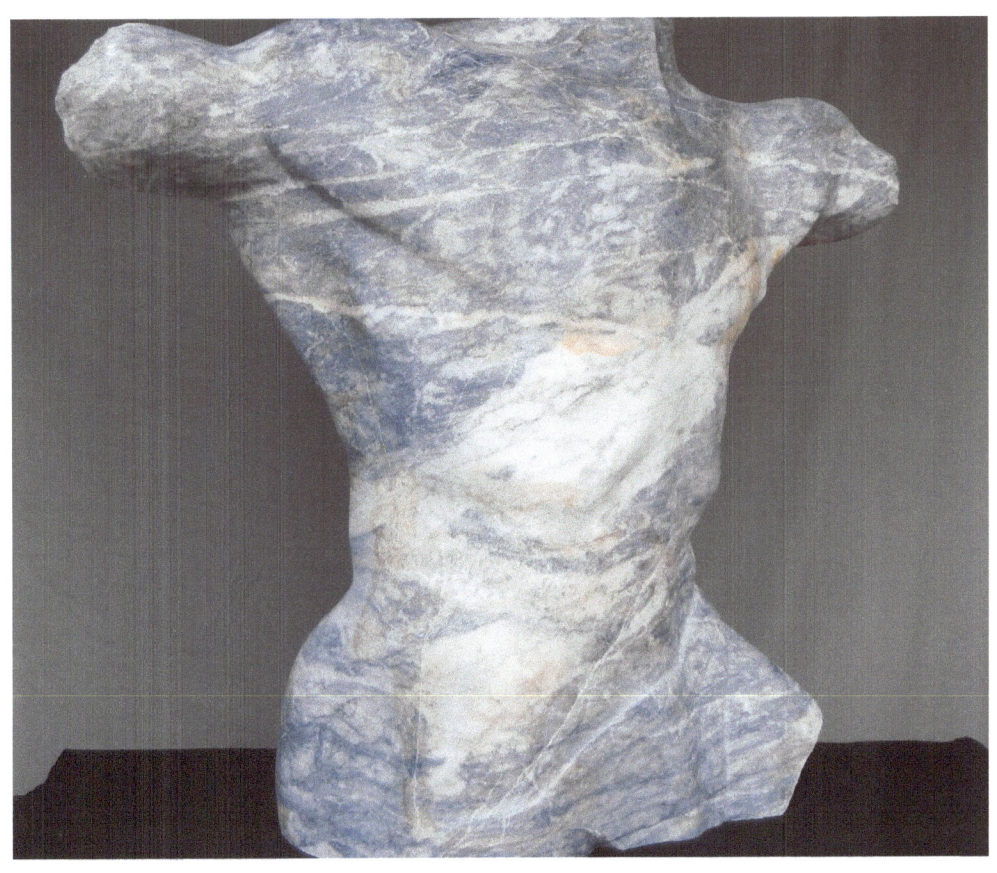

Torso One, Honey I'm Home
Dan Irvine
32" x 36"
Okanagan marble & 24c gold leaf

An exploration in neo-classical revival(gag me) or a playful twist on an ancient art form?
... you decide.

Dan McCormack

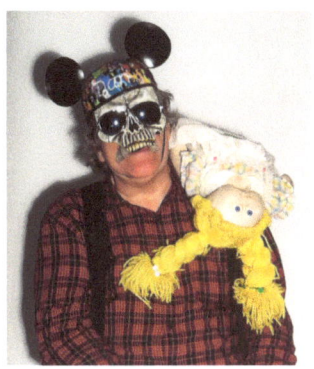

From 1962 – 1970, I studied photography at the Institute of Design and the School of the Art Institute of Chicago. I began photographing the nude with Wendy, my wife while in graduate school. I won a NYSCA CAPS Photography Fellowship. With that series, in 1989, I produced a monograph, "BODY LIGHT - Passages in a Relationship". In 2009, I won the Ultimate Eye Foundation's grant for Figurative Photography. For over forty years, I explored various techniques and processes while photographing the nude as a central theme. I currently head Photography at Marist College in Poughkeepsie, NY.

http://www.danmccormack.net

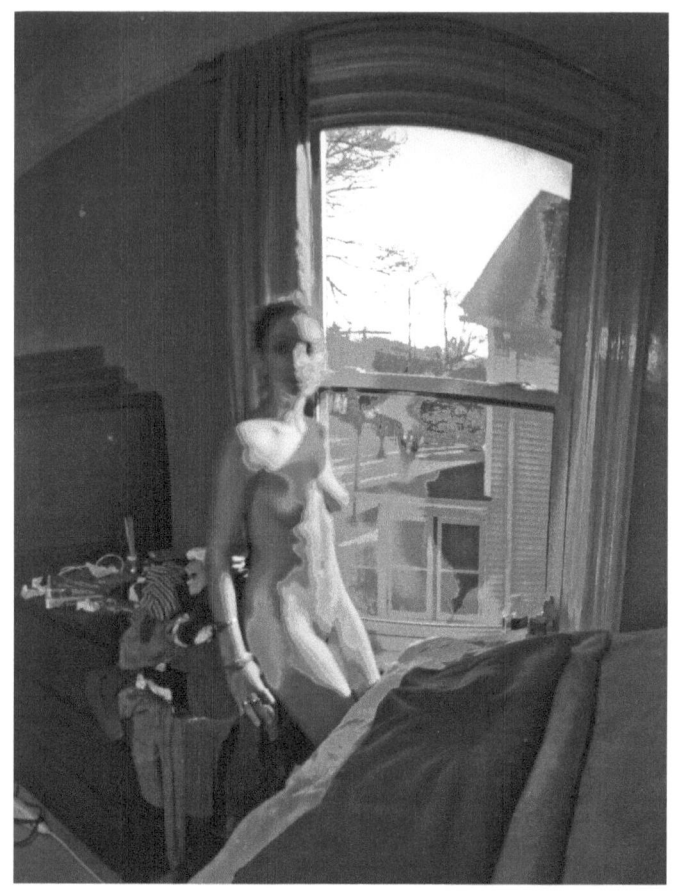

Eva_B_12-03-11--12AB
Dan McCormack
20" x 16"
Pinhole Camera - Digital Pigment Print

I am photographing in the privacy of Eva's bedroom
and celebrating the warmth of the sunlight on a cold day.

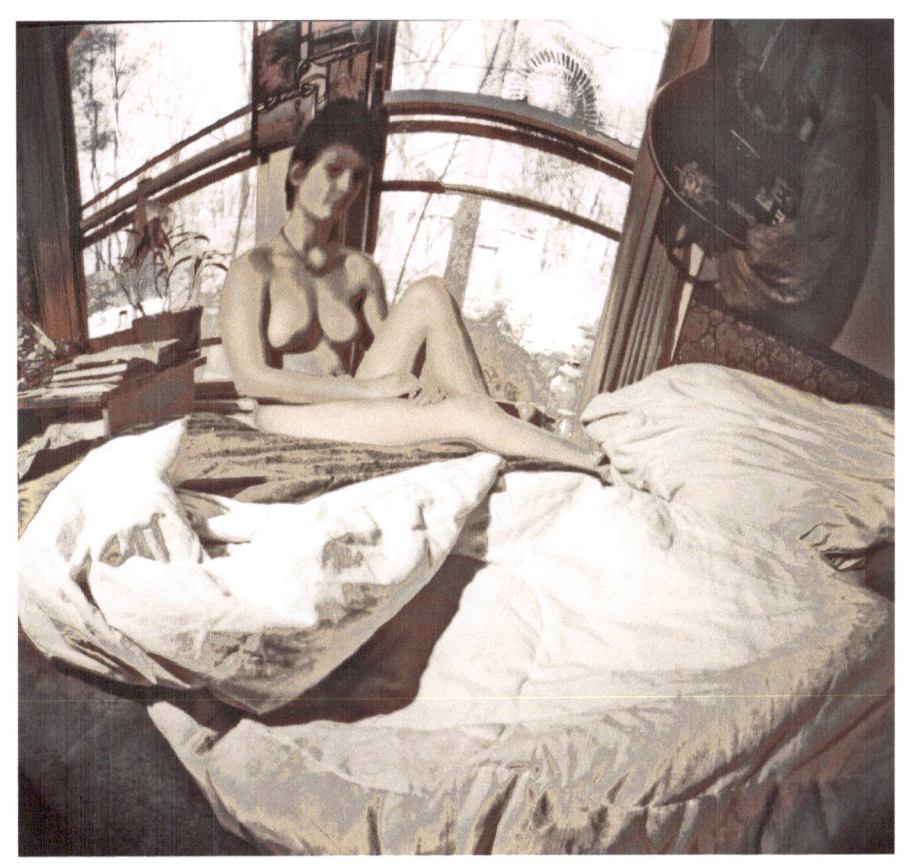

Lana_H_11-19-11--11AB
Dan McCormack
20" x 16"
Pinhole Camera - Digital Pigment Print

I am photographing in the privacy of Lana's bedroom
and celebrating the intimate moments shared.

Dongmin Lai

I was born in China and came to Canada in 1991. I finished my art training in Beijing China. I have been an artist for about 40 years. I am now living Kelowna since I came to Canada 20 years ago.

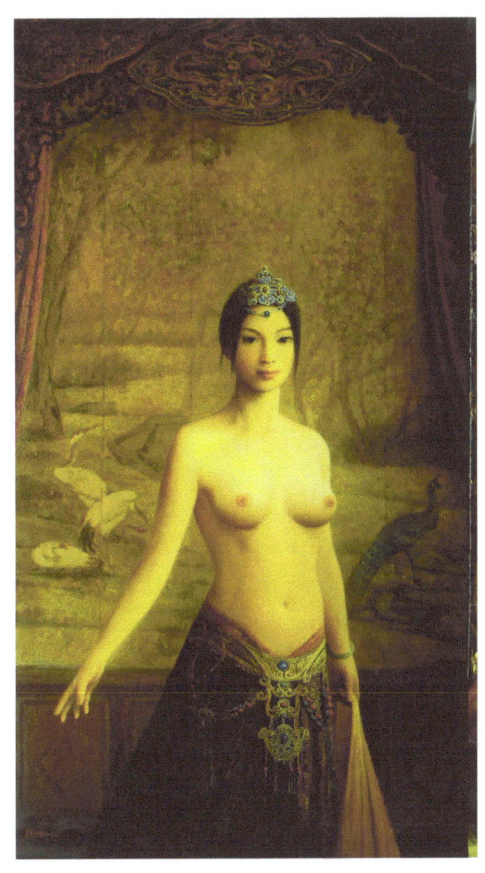

Jia (The Beautiful)
Dongmin Lai
44" x 26"
Oil on Canvas

----------------a mystery ancient Chinese beauty.

Ellen Houben

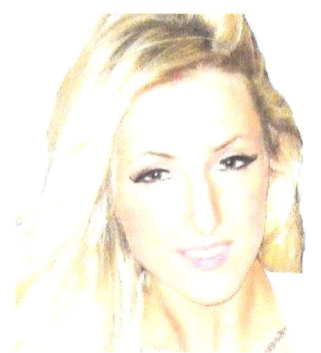

Ellen Houben was born and raised in Calgary Alberta. She began sketching as a child, and was encouraged by family and friends for years to flex her artistic muscle. Ellen moved to Kelowna in 2010, and it was here that she finally found herself immersed in ideas and expressing them with paint. Ellen has been largely self taught; with limited formal education in the arts. She found her inspiration around the same time she was expecting her baby girl who will be a year old in April 2012.

http://www.ellenhouben.com

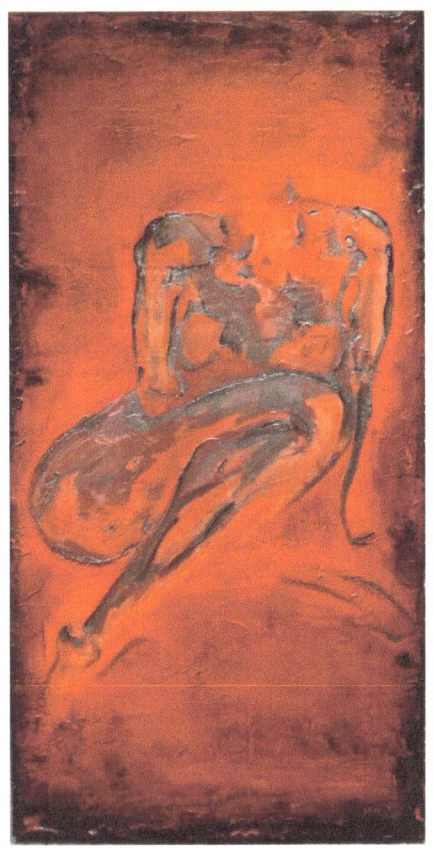

Red Room
Ellen Houben
48" x 24"
Acrylic and Mixed Media on Canvas

If not doomed, not forbidden, must be daring, must be dire.

Gail Marie Kern

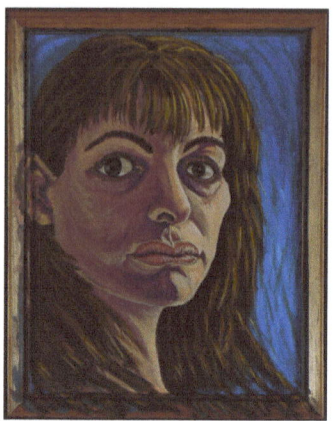

Gail Marie Kern lives in St. Paul Minnesota with her husband, several pets and too many plants. She enjoys paint and drawing comics.

http://MNartists.org/Gail_Kern

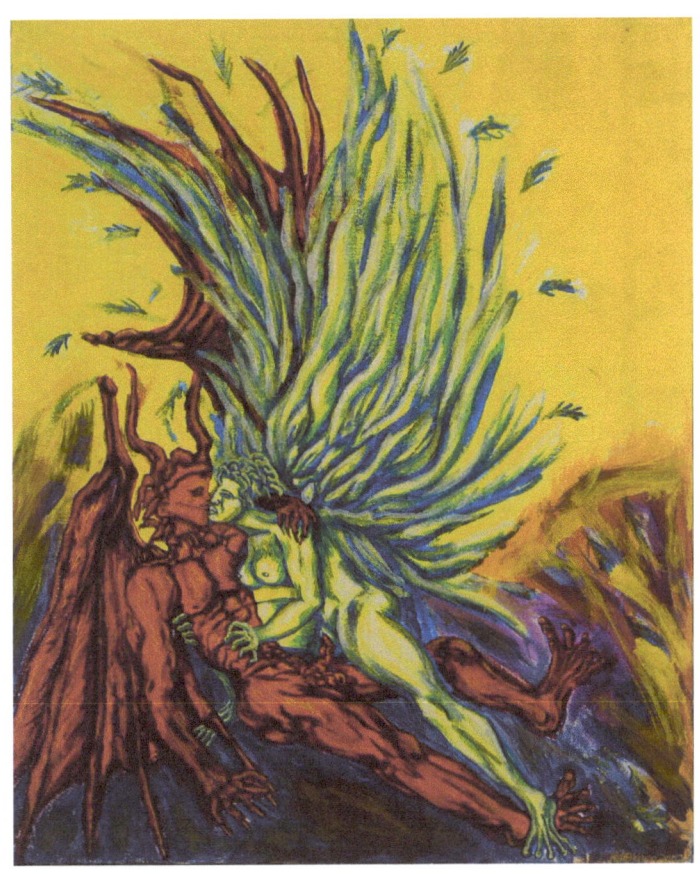

Genesis II
Gail Marie Kern
24" x 18"
Acrylic on Canvas

The boy Demon lets the girl Angel "have her way with him".

Gary Mitchell

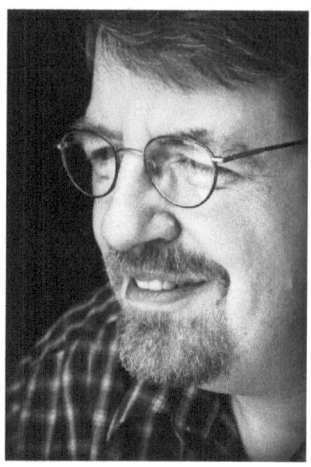

Gary Mitchell has been a photographer most of his life, and in 2006 turned his attention to artistic nude and erotic photography. He enjoys live music, films, guidebooks, and collects photography books. He enjoys exchanging prints with his fellow photographers and supporting their work. He lives in Dayton, Ohio, USA and runs a small advertising business. In January 2011, he stopped watching television and following politics and current events and feels much better for it.

http://garym.com
http://garymphoto.tumblr.com
http://about.me/garymitchell

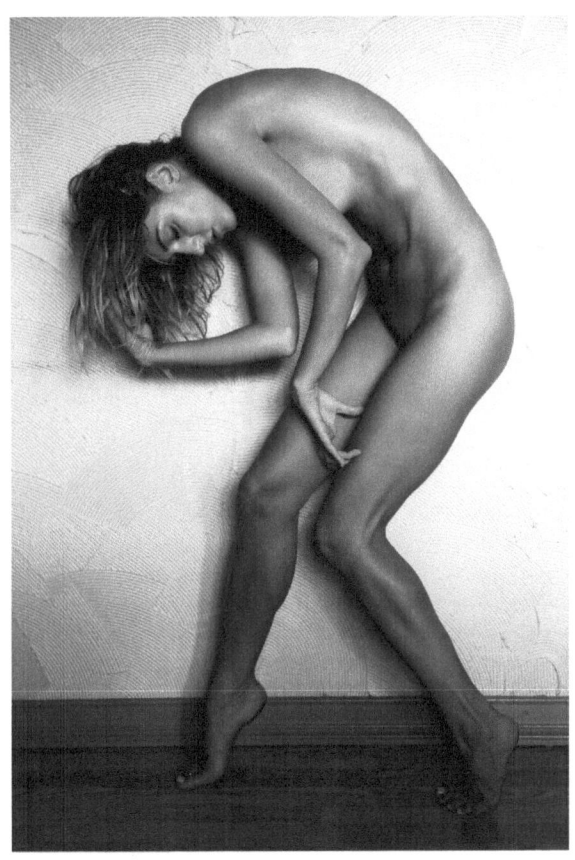

Bewegungsstudie
Gary Mitchell
24" x 18"
Photograph

The tension, abandon and emotion of the gesture betrays the perfection of model's form.

Gerry Greengrove

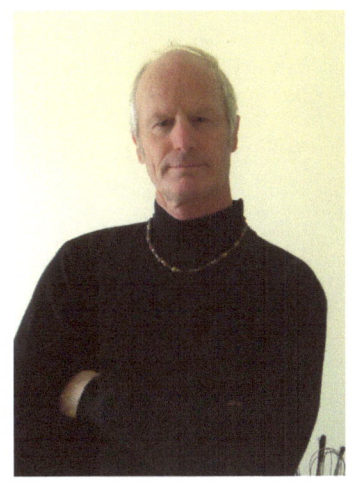

Ten years ago I went to the VCAC to study wood carving but found myself in the pottery studio. Ceramics became my obsession for the next ten years. I have studied under Gail Woodhouse and J Diller and am a member of the Okanagan Potters Group. I have been lifecasting for the past 2 years and am a member of The international Lifecasting Association. My casts have been exhibited in several Okanagan venues...

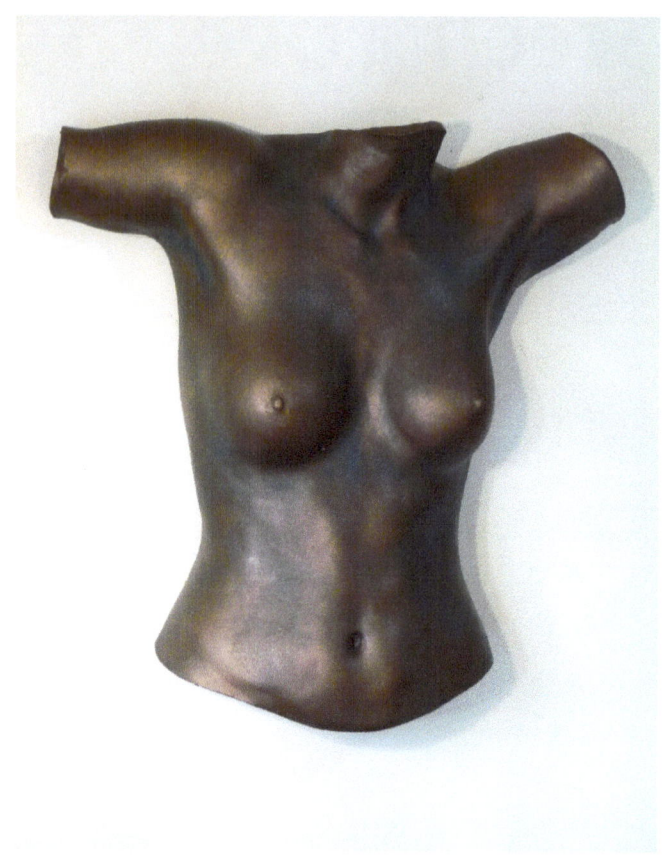

Dignity
Gerry Greengrove
24" x 24"
Hydrostone Life Casting

... young , shy, but sensuous, she's a dreamer holding onto innocence.

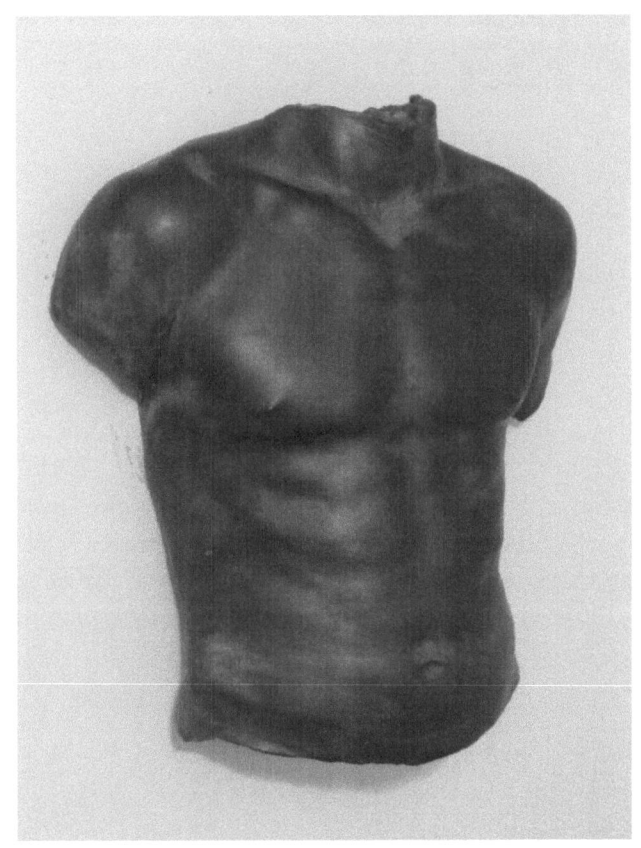

Strength
Gerry Greengrove
24" x 24"
Hydrostone Life Casting

... this piece reeks of testosterone, masculine and virile.

Gracie Ackerman

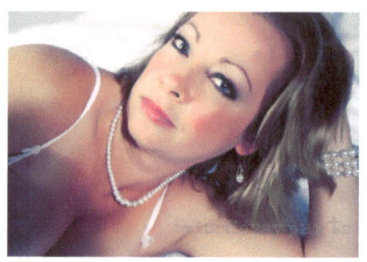

My name is Gracie Ackerman; I am an untrained artist/writer/poet. I have lived in and around the Okanagan Valley since 1983. I went to George Elliot Secondary School in Winfield BC, I then went Okanagan School of Hairdressing in Kelowna and then on to Business College. I am and advocate for women's rights towards freedom of expression and sexuality. I am the proud mother of three young children, Tessa 12, Robyn 10 and Tyler who will soon be 5.

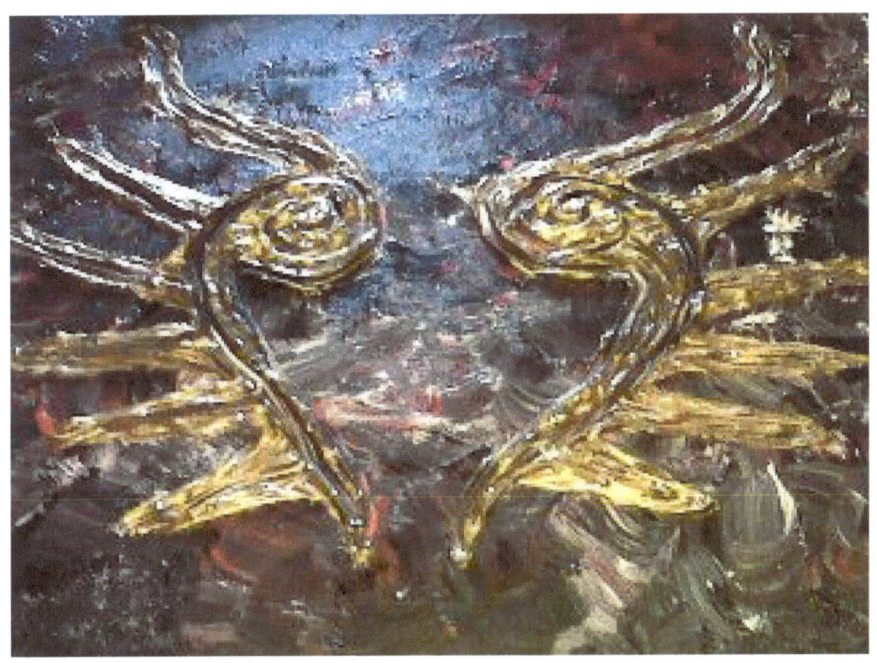

Wings of Eros
Gracie Ackerman
24" x 36"
Mixed Media on Canvas

This is a very ancient symbol...originating from Greece...this god is also known as Cupid.

Jackie Champion

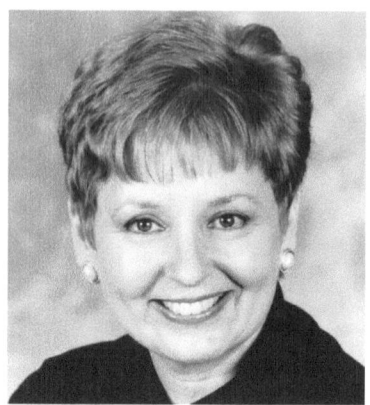

I was born in Vancouver, BC, and received my education at UBC. Both my father, who painted in oils, and my grandmother, who used watercolours, influenced my decision to become an artist. I lived in Europe for two years, visiting many museums and galleries. I am very proud of my three children and four grandsons. Painting, tennis, gardening and travel are my main passions.

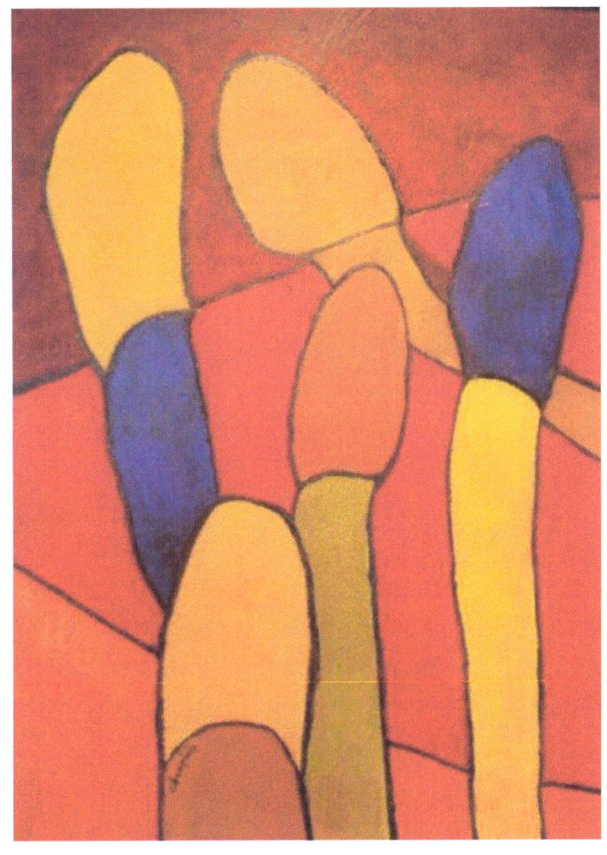

Come and Light My Fire
Jackie Champion
38" x 26"
Acrylic on Canvas

One evening feeling particularly seductive and wickedly sexy I drew some matchsticks, which inflamed the ache and raw animal instinct I needed to act out an erotic and risque moment!

Jaime Seward

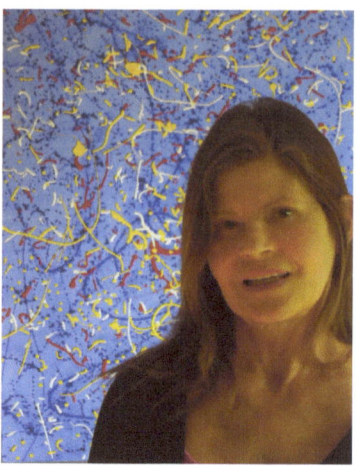

Intuitiveness, truth, and a love for nature, animals and her fellow humans , have made Seward the impressive person she is today. An award winning artist, she is well schooled in all media having had shows through out the Okanagan Valley and beyond. Born into a large family in Manitoba, she talks of sketching on the backs of envelopes and filling chalk boards at school with her early childhood works. "To this day a white canvas or a blank piece of paper excites me and gets my mind racing. I was told many times that I have a natural gift." Seward lives in the North Okanagan on her retreat acreage where she paints, teaches and invites others to come create with her.

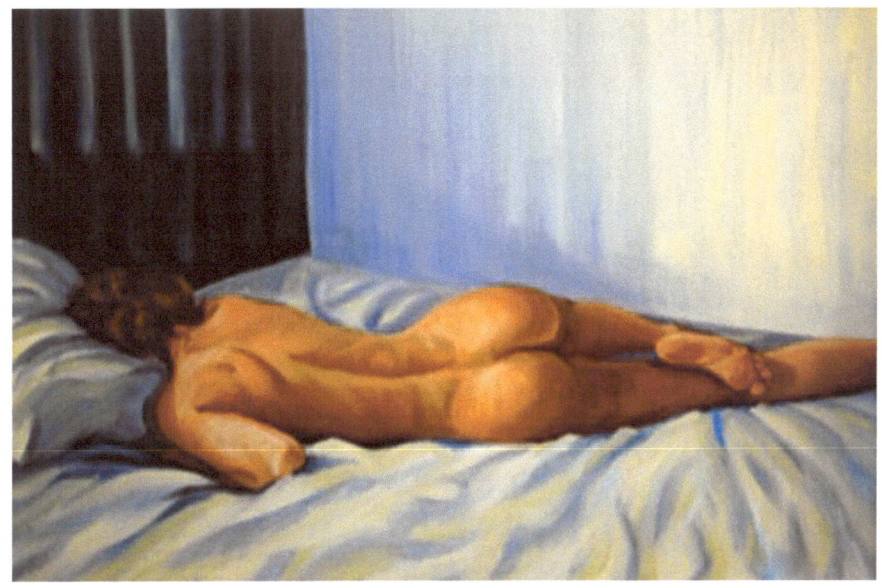

Blue Nude
Jaime Seward
24" x 30"
Oil on Canvas

I painted the "Blue Nude" in order to evoke anticipation and/or imagination
as to what happened just prior or what is about to...

Jaine Buse

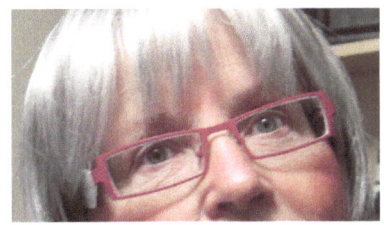

Jaine is an avid and continuous learner and practitioner in the arts who has rebranded her skills after spending 25 years in managing her own Human Resource Management Company. Her love of nature, cycling, hiking, travelling the world and people watching   allows her to capture images to stimulate her creativity.

She is involved in art programs for Hospice clients and their families plus a board member of the Kelowna Livessence Figurative Drawing Society.

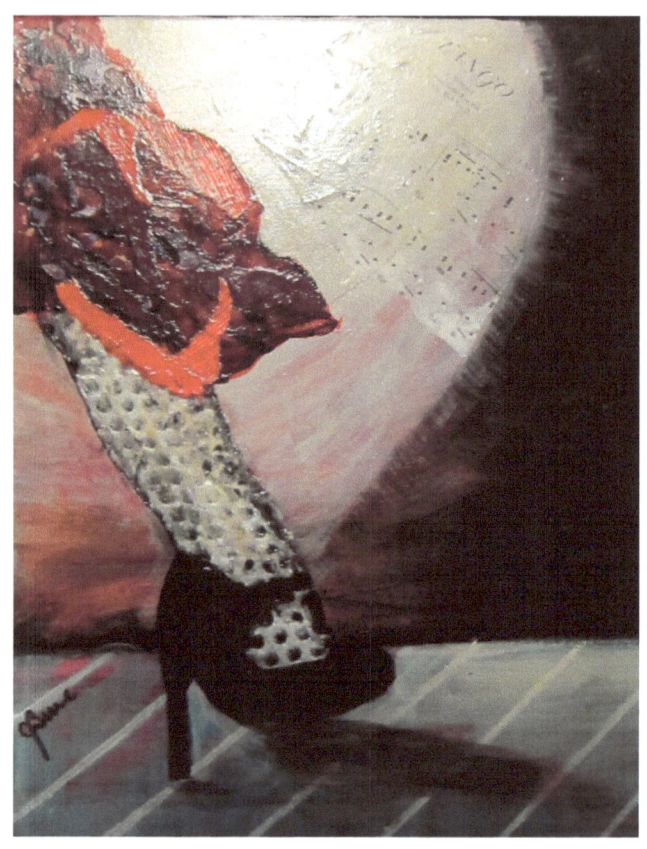

Tango I
Jaine Buse
15" x 12"
Acrylic and Collage

Notes Staccato Bodies Heat Breasts Touch Breasts Thighs Brush Thighs Hearts Race….

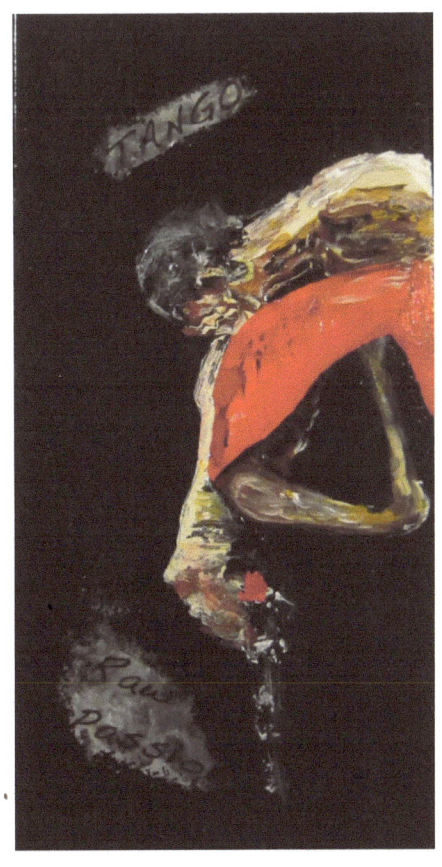

Tango II
Jaine Buse
25" x 13"
Acrylic and Collage

Notes Staccato Bodies Heat Breasts Touch Breasts Thighs Brush Thighs Hearts Race….

James Postill

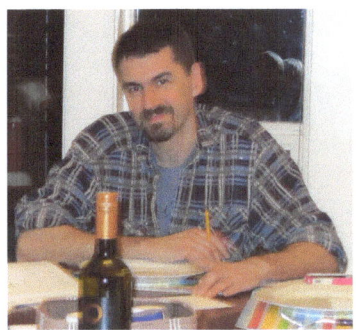

James Postill, B.F.A., is a practicing artist in Vernon who paints oils and frescoes, and is artist in residence at Vernon's Caetani Cultural Centre. As resident artist, he has completed a casein and pigment mural on their straw bale studio.   He has been fortunate to have been mentored by artists such as Jack Shadbolt, Ken Kirkby, Rick Bond, and fresco master Father Dunstan Massey. His work is collected internationally, and has received a lot of recognition from both art galleries, and the community. He shares his knowledge through teaching art to people of all ages.

http://www.jamespostill.blogspot.com

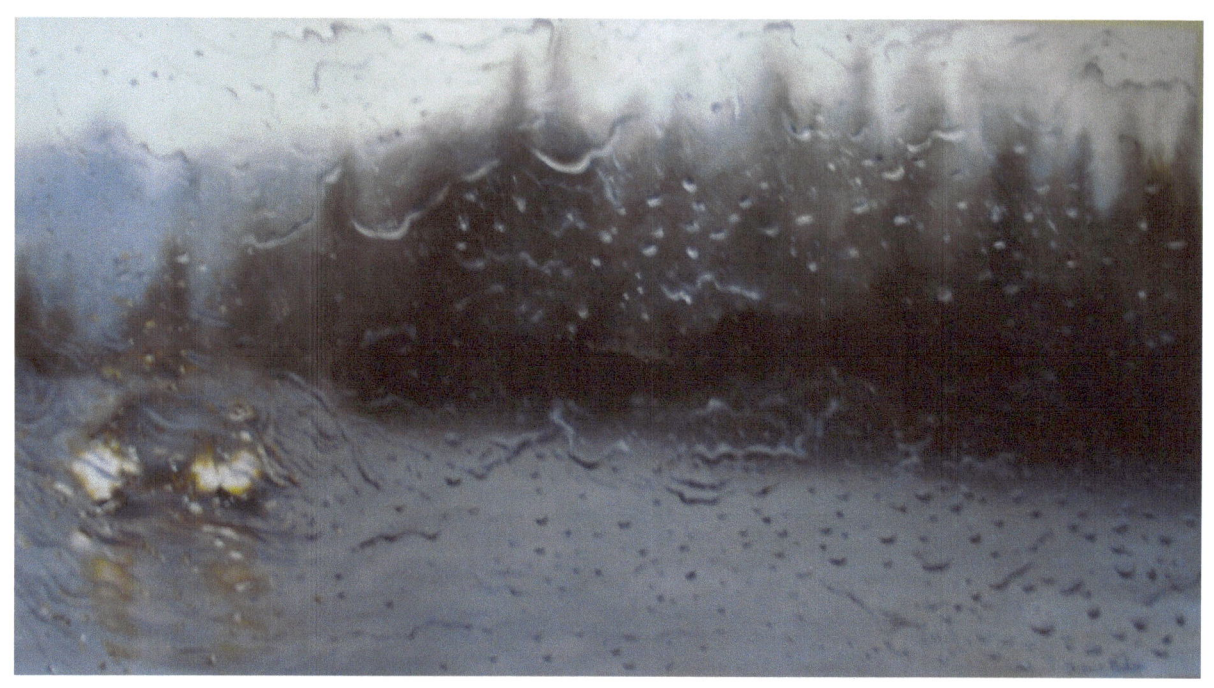

Highway
James Postill
26" x 48"
Oil on Panel

rain, shower, downpour
streams of water run through our lives
my senses aroused

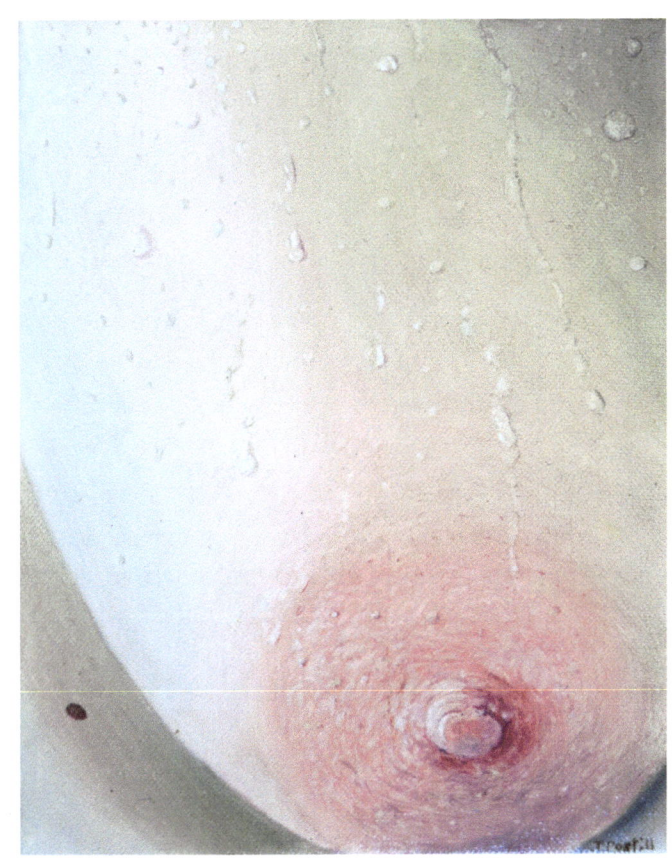

Blush
James Postill
10" x 8"
Oil on Canvas

rain, shower, downpour
streams of water run through our lives
my senses aroused

Jeffrey Bain

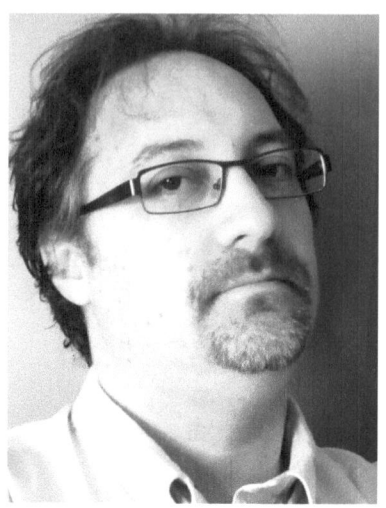

Jeff Bain was born in 1965. He was lucky enough to have rich experiences in the diverse areas of western and northern Canada, and was born in an age of great promise where technology seemed to offer something to those willing to take the risk and dare to dream. His fascination with art began at an early age with the appreciation of the beauty of the world around him. He enjoys drawing people the most. He also composes music, but his acquaintances always say, This is my friend, Jeff. He is an artist.

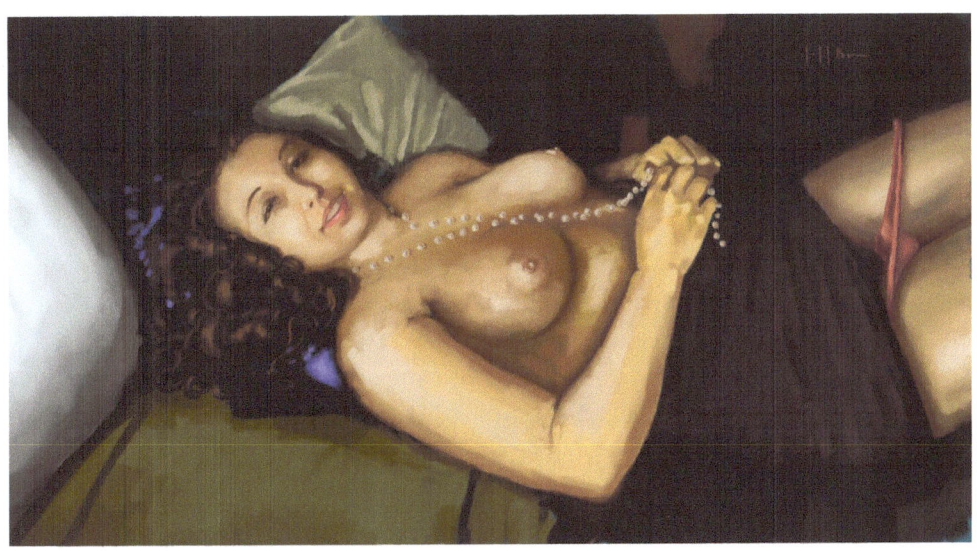

Pearles for Odette
Jeffrey Bain
11" x 20"
Digital Painting on Canvas 1/1

She helps me forget.

Jennifer Burrows

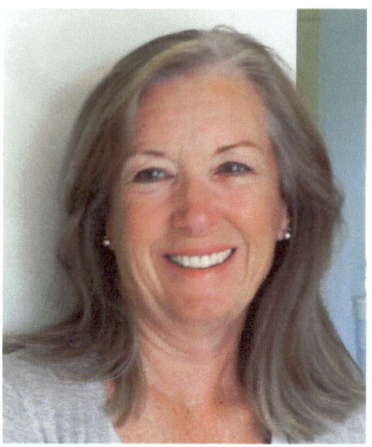

Jennifer was born and raised in Montreal and earned degrees from Concordia and Simon Fraser Universities. Following eight years with large corporations in Montreal and Vancouver, Jennifer taught full-time (including art) in Vernon for the next twenty-eight years.

Along the way, Jennifer visited a Robert Genn exhibit in Kelowna that sparked her passion to paint and directly influenced her philosophy and her style. Jennifer's work has been displayed in some Okanagan galleries and successfully juried into several exhibits in the Kelowna area.

http://www.jenniferburrowsart.com

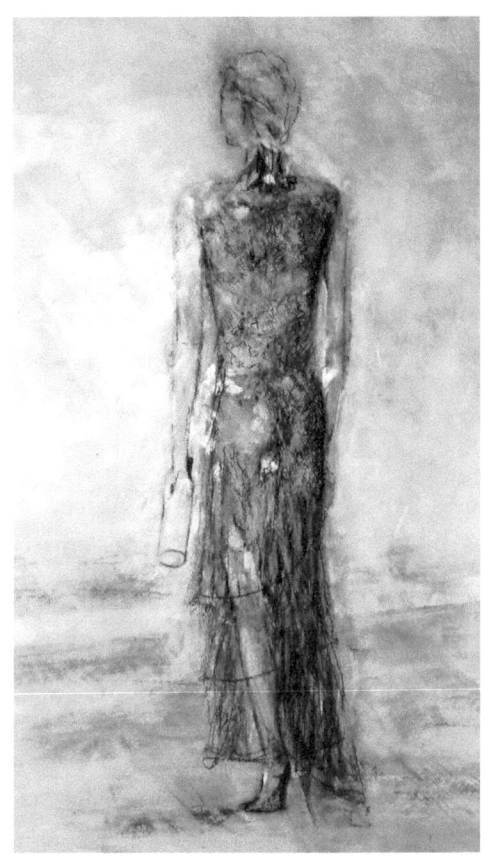

Alluring Lace
Jennifer Burrows
31" x 22"
Charcoal and Acrylic on Watercolour Paper

As promised, she wore black lace, hopeful that tonight
would satisfy every desire she had imagined.

Jessica Klein

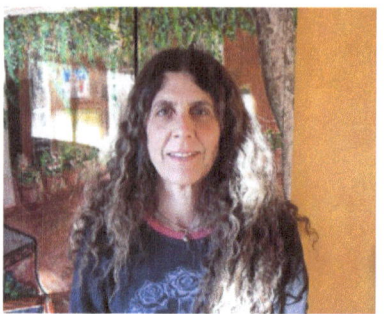

Jessica loves spending time with friends, her family, working for peace, community, and animal rights. In her newly built studio, on her organic family farm, she is exploring her creative energy, painting, and revisiting j ewelry making.

This is her first work in the erotic realm, delving into family secrets. Her use of gold leaf and three dimensions, as well as photos, has a lot to do with her 25 years' experience as a jeweler and photographer.

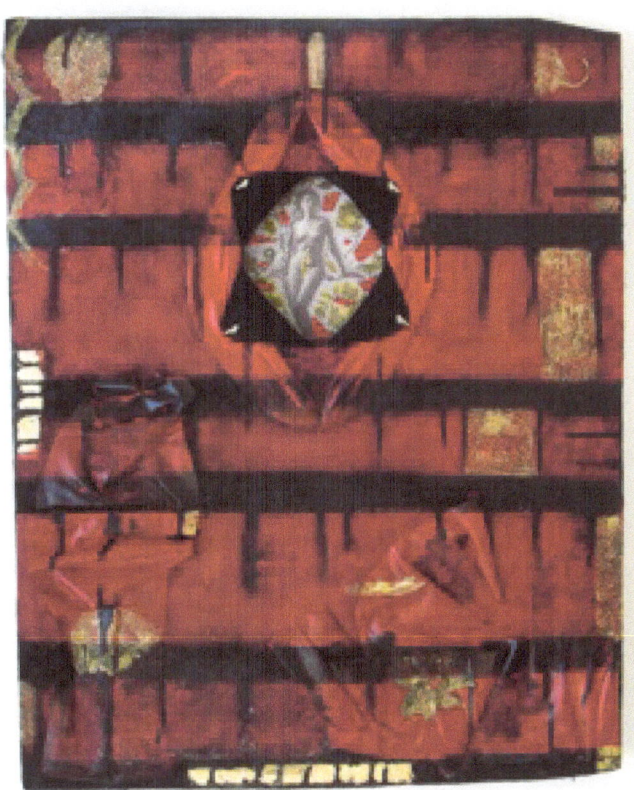
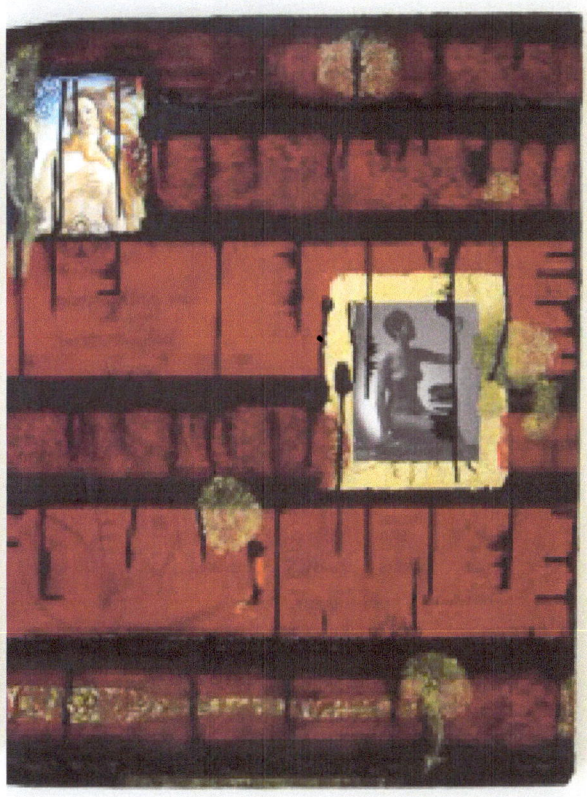

Venus Secret and Teddy's Secret Venus(Diptych)
Jessica Klein
31" x 25" each
Acrylic, Material, Lace, Gold Leaf, Mixed Media on Plywood

Jessika Von Innerebner

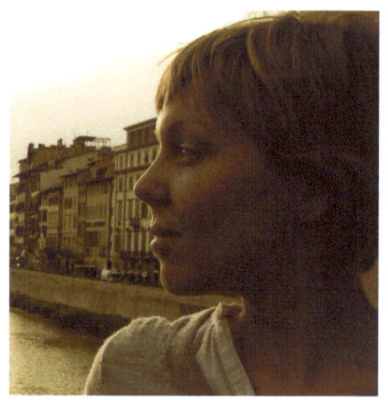

Jessika's an illustrator / animator who creates mad and crazy educational fun for amazing people. Currently she works as head art person for Mathtoons Media. She has 14 years experience in the field and has amassed a decent sized hill of knowledge. On downtime Jessika loves to sketch, illustrate and can be found running in circles, she loves to travel and laugh with friends...sometimes at them! She has a fish named Sashimi and fully appreciates the irony.

http://www.kartoonkid.com

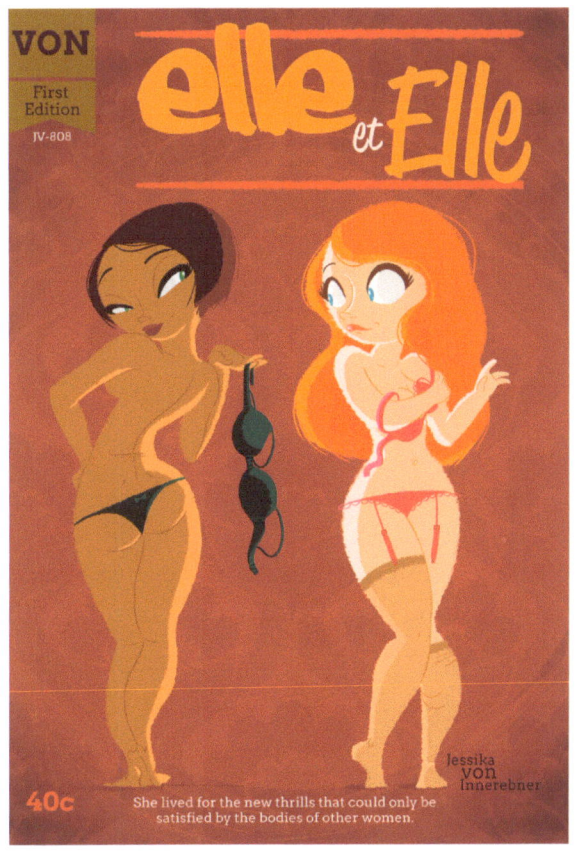

Pulp Fiction
Jessika von Innerebner
36" x 24"
Digital Painting

This piece celebrates pulp novels of the past with a cheeky illustration.

Jim Britton

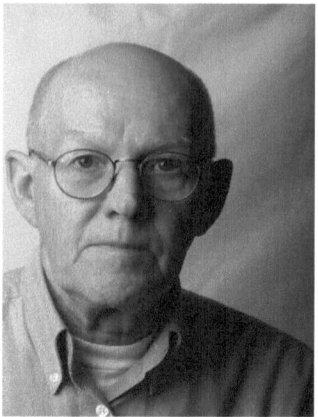

Jim Britton is a retired commercial portrait photographer. His photographic career began when he was still too young to go to school, and his uncle taught him to work in a darkroom. This life long addiction has served him well as he found that people would pay him to do what he loved to do - taking pictures of people. Jim has retired from photographing weddings, but not from exploring the artistic side of photography.

http://www.pbase.com/jimbritton

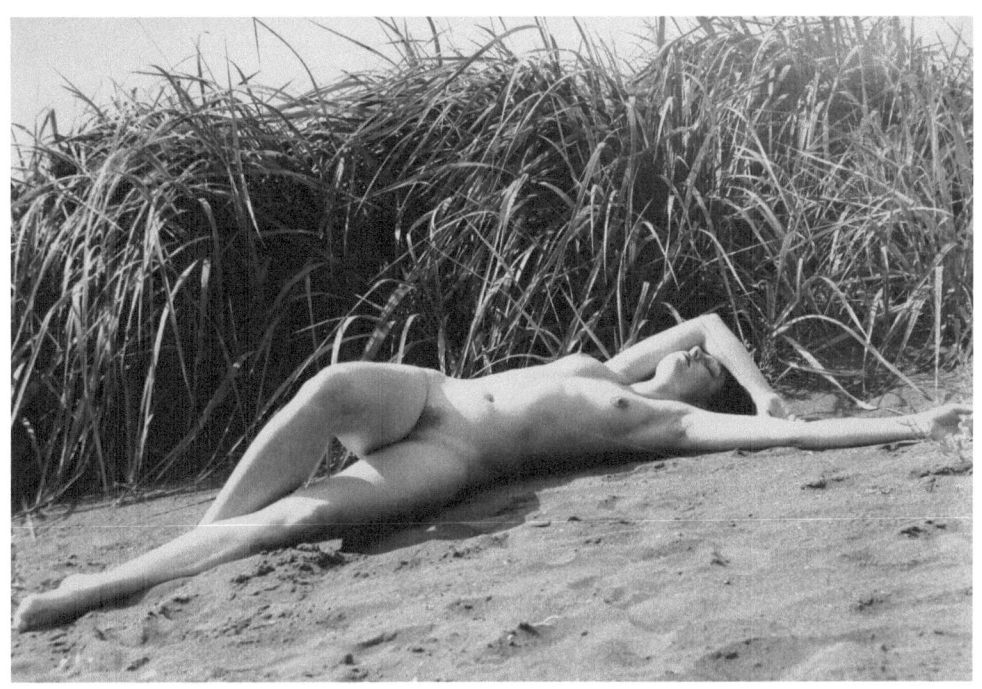

On the Beach
Jim Britton
16" x 20"
Sepia Toned Silver Emulsion Photograph

Alive she felt - exposed to the warmth of the sun and to whoever cast eyes upon her.

Joyce Krenn

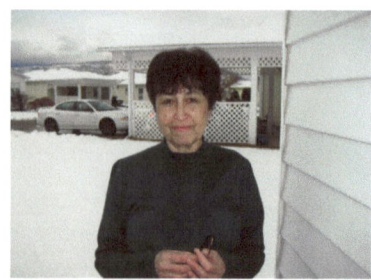

Joyce grew up in the Okanagan in a rural setting surrounded by the beauty of orchards and gardens. This inbred love of nature is the soul of her painting which she is able to presue now that she is retired from a nursing career. She continues to take classes from different local artists and sells at various local venues.

http://www.joycekrennartwork.ca

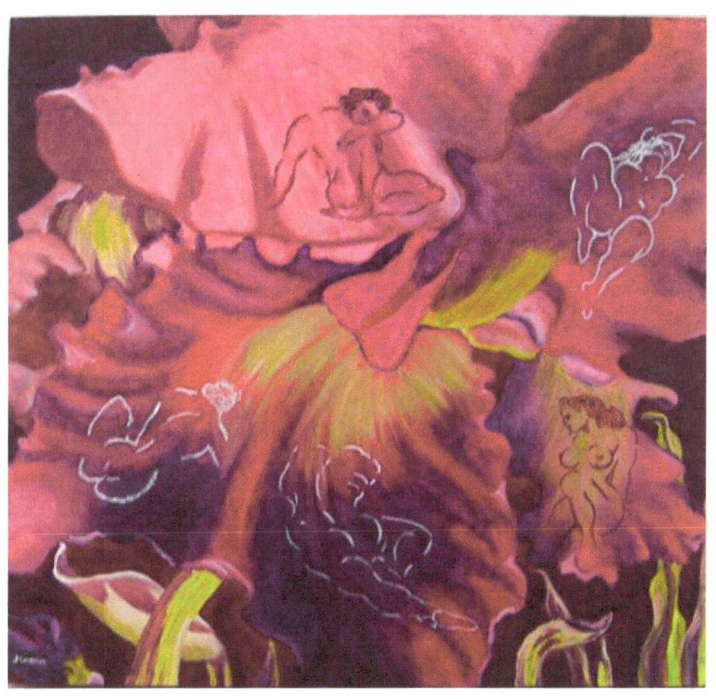

Greek Nudes on Iris
Joyce Krenn
24" x 24"
Oil on Canvas

Old Greek gods of love, Eros, Aphrodite-like figures enjoy the sensuous curves of the iris petals.

Julia Trops

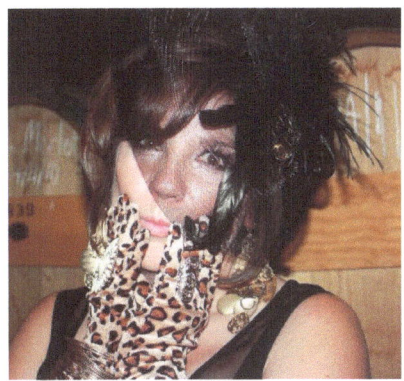

Julia Trops is an international multi-disciplinary artist having sold over 1100 artworks worldwide since 2004. Retaining the focus, work ethic and integrity from her 12 year career in the military, this decorated artist is very involved in the Okanagan art community. Julia is one of the original organizers of the Okanagan Erotic Art Show and has carried on the event on her own since 2009. Livessence Society for Figurative Artists and Models was born from Julia's life drawing sessions started in 2003 and won the 2010 Central Okanagan Community Group Arts Award. Julia is represented in the Okanagan by Gallery Odin at Silver Star Ski Resort, and at Creatio Ex Nihilo. In 2011, Julia was nominated for both the Okanagan Arts Award for Visual Artist, and for the Kelowna Civic Awards - Honour in the Arts.

http://www.juliatrops.com

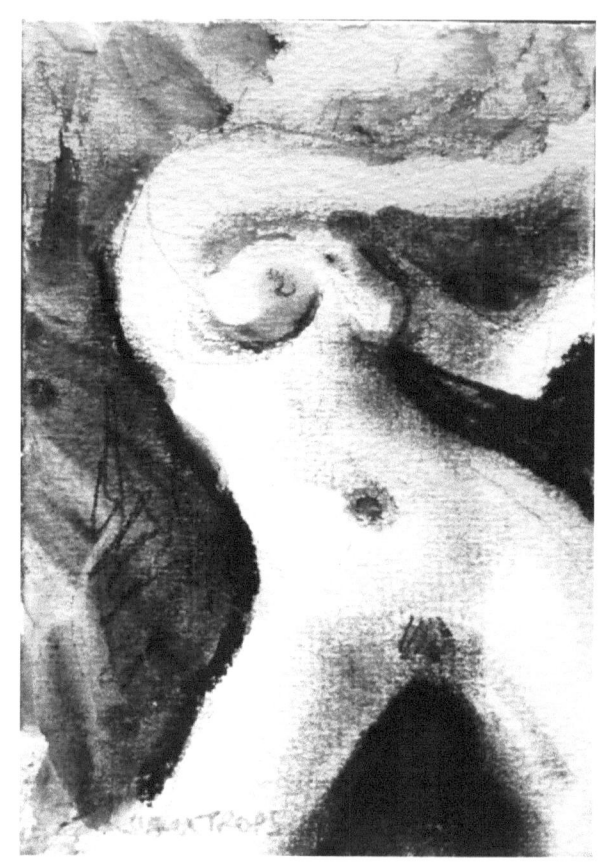

Finger Painting I
Julia Trops
14" x 11"
Charcoal and Graphite

Wet fingers.

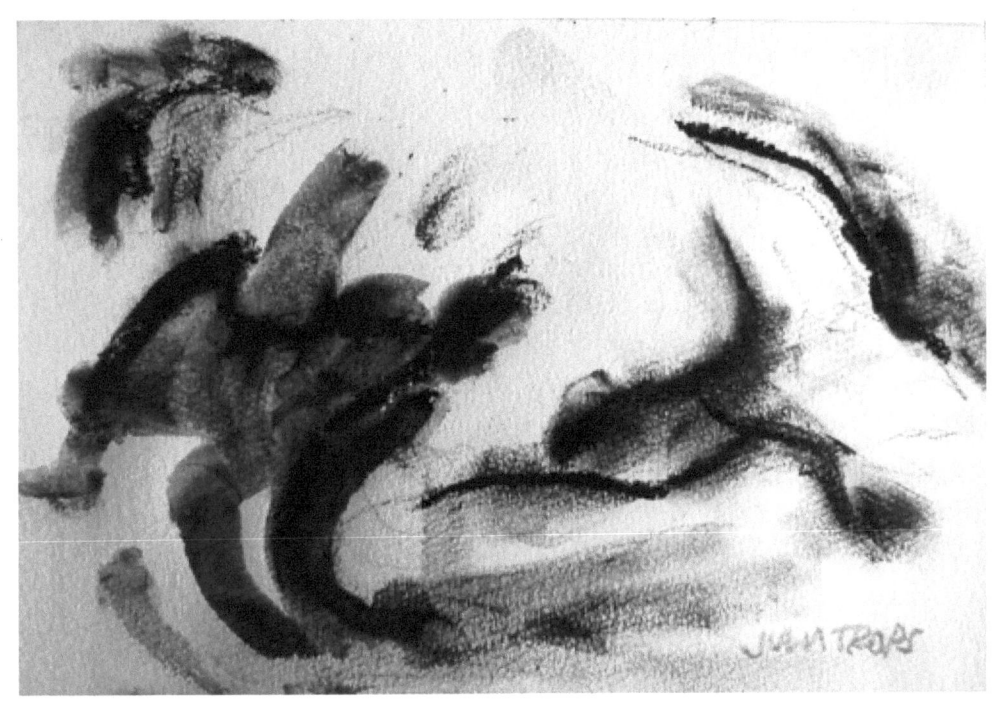

Finger Painting I
Julia Trops
14" x 11"
Charcoal and Graphite

Gripping.

June Seed

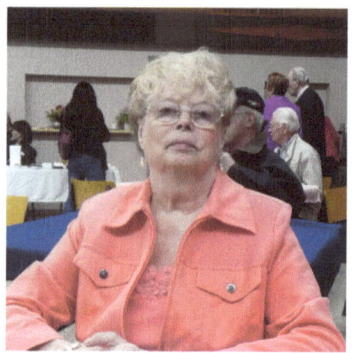

June's involvement in the arts started at an early age. She started singing in church and school choirs, learned to dance and practiced her artistic talents in school. After school in Ottawa she moved to Vancouver. There she joined the Vancouver Opera Society and sang in a number of operas in the Queen Elizabeth Theater. In Lake Country, she has continued to paint and exhibit, June is a past director of the Kelowna Art Gallery and is a member of the Art Walk Organizing Committee, the Municipal Art Advisory Commission and is on the Board of the Lake Country Art Gallery.

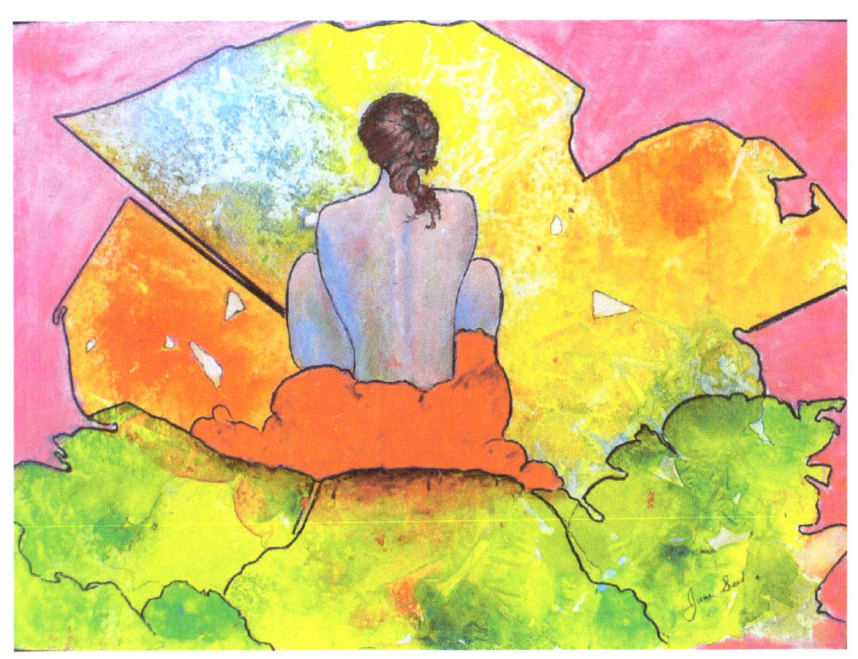

Contemplation
June Seed
18" x 24"
Acrylic on Canvas

Kai Eckhardt

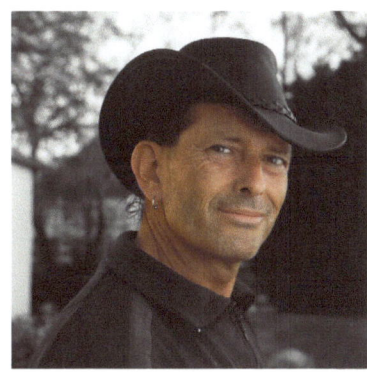

I was born 1960 in Kiel, a town in the North of Germany, where I was also raised. I am self-taught working as a freelance Photodesigner and Artist with my own Studio and a small Gallery in Nortorf, Germany. Starting with the analogue photography as a kid, I'm using now the digital technique. After years of experience with different directions of motives (landscapes, architecture, people) is my special focus now on the erotic and fine art nude photography.

http://www.ke-erotic.com

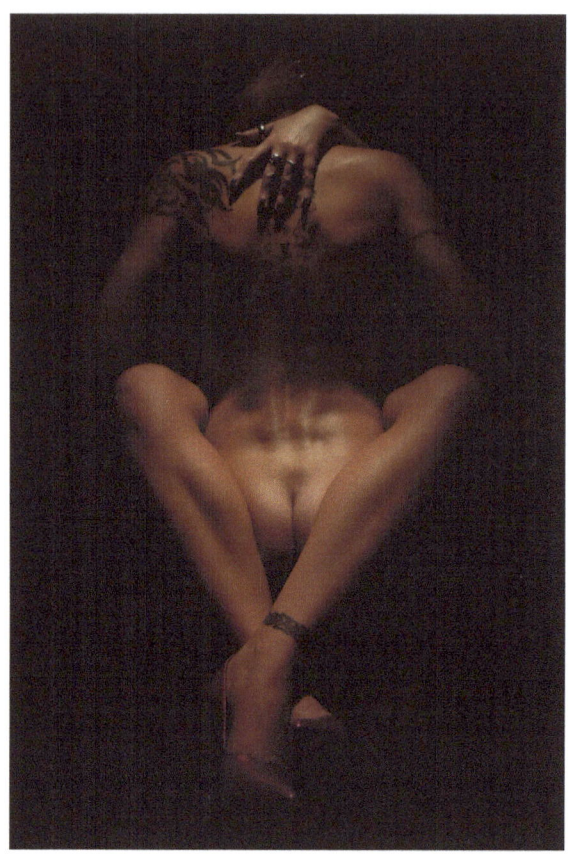

Excite
Kai Eckhardt (check spelling)
24" x 18"
Photography

Don't fear about fingernails – but can you hear them scratching on the skin?

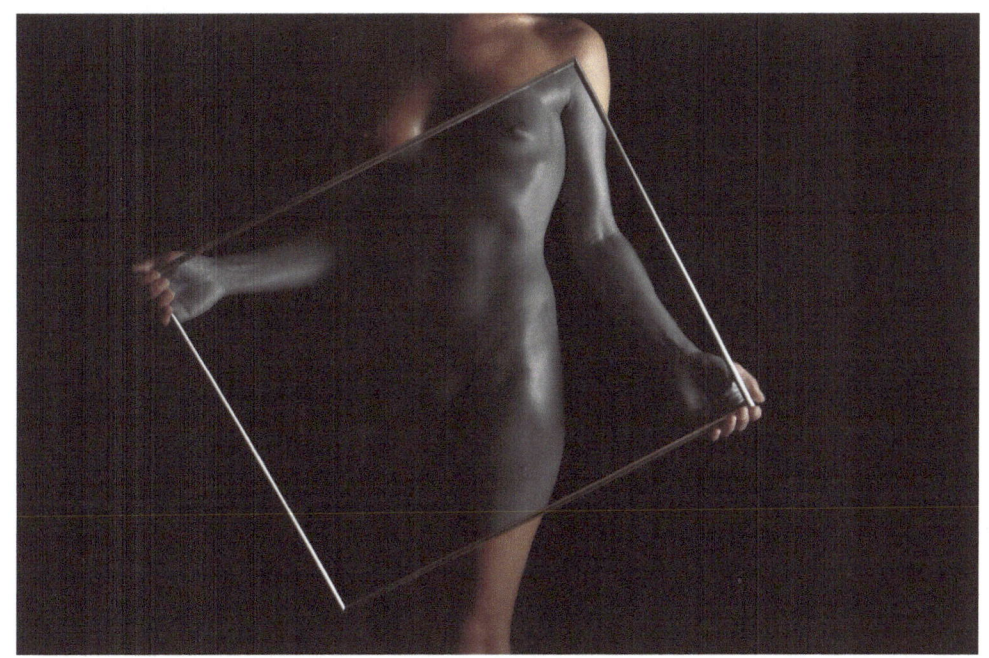

The Frame
Kai Eckhardt
24" x 18"
Photography

Is the body inside the frame just looking colder – or is that an imagine?

Karla Warkotsch

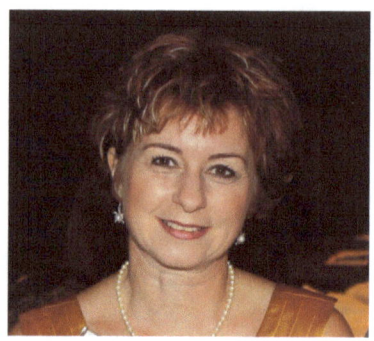

Karla Warkotsch grew up in the Lower Mainland and after two years studying fine arts at Kwantlen College, she decided a health care career was an easier way to make a living. Schooling finished and family grown Karla returned to her first love and joined a Kelowna based pottery studio. Classes were taken and workshops attended resulting in creations for local shows and sales. Looking for another challenge she finished a Masters degree from Royal Roads University and on completion in 2009, changed artistic direction to take Acrylic Painting classes on Tuesday nights. With a progressive busy health care career Karla looks forward to the time when Tuesday nights and weekends aren't the only time to paint!

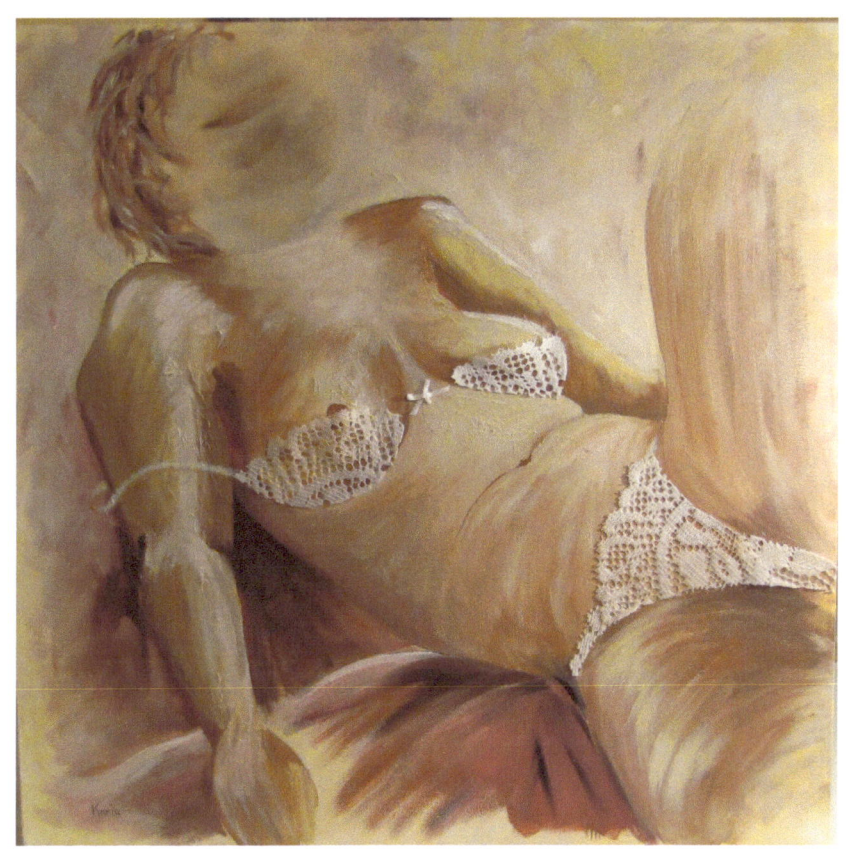

Enough!
Karla Warkotsch
24" x 24"
Mixed Media on Canvas

Lying at ease, her thoughts cry out– enough!

Kendi Clearwater

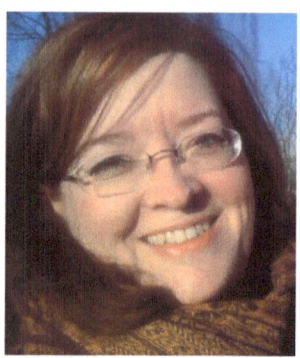

I am the daughter of Joy, mother of three amazing young women, sister to four crazy, inspiring women, and grandmother of one astounding toddler. I love the beauty of women and am inpired by the complexity of human relationships. I have now reached the age in my life where I am not afraid to own my own truth. I have a vision of what I wish to create, in images, words and song, and so, like you - I find my way.

Now 50, 5 ft 6ish, I have lived in the Okanagan for 4 years, .. the rest changes without notice.

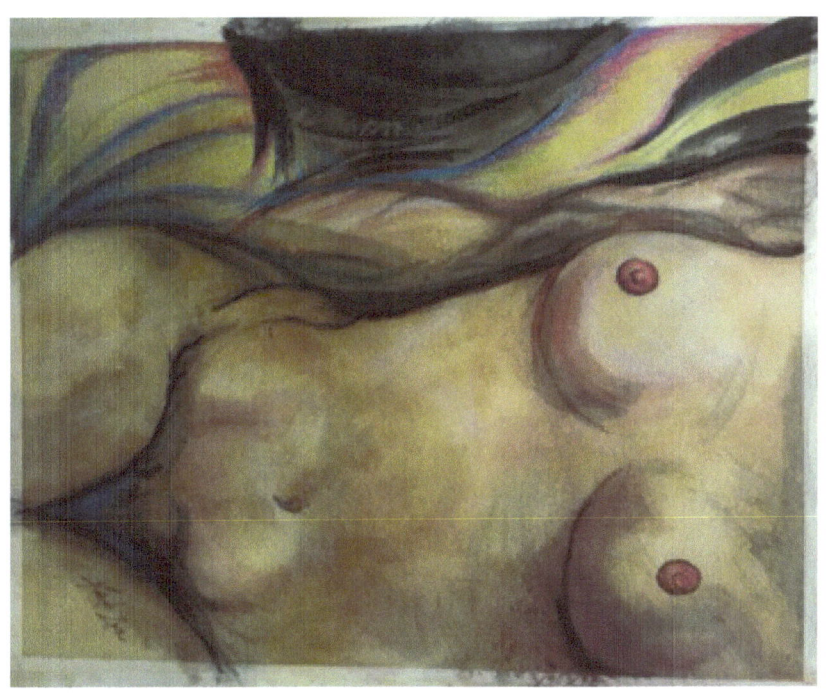

Kindling
Kendi Clearwater
Watercolour, Tea and Pencil Crayon
18" x 24"

Do you long for moment your lover's alchemy crosses the danger zone?

Kimberly Walker

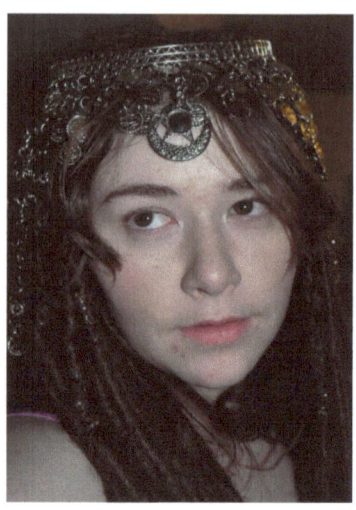

Kimberly resides in Kelowna BC and has a BFA from UBC-O. She likes sex and has compiled a list of her favourite euphemisms, which, given the open nature of this show, she feels compelled to share...
SO here we go:

sexual intercourse or relations, coitus, happy hour, mating, copulation, intimacy, lovemaking, coupling, shacking up, screwing, shafting, shagging, cottaging, leg over, "how's your father", ROMP, toss, boink, horny time, knock boots, get busy, horizontal dance, bumping uglies, knocking boots, getting it on, fornication, riding the bologna pony, hot beef injection..

http://www.lacepistol.com

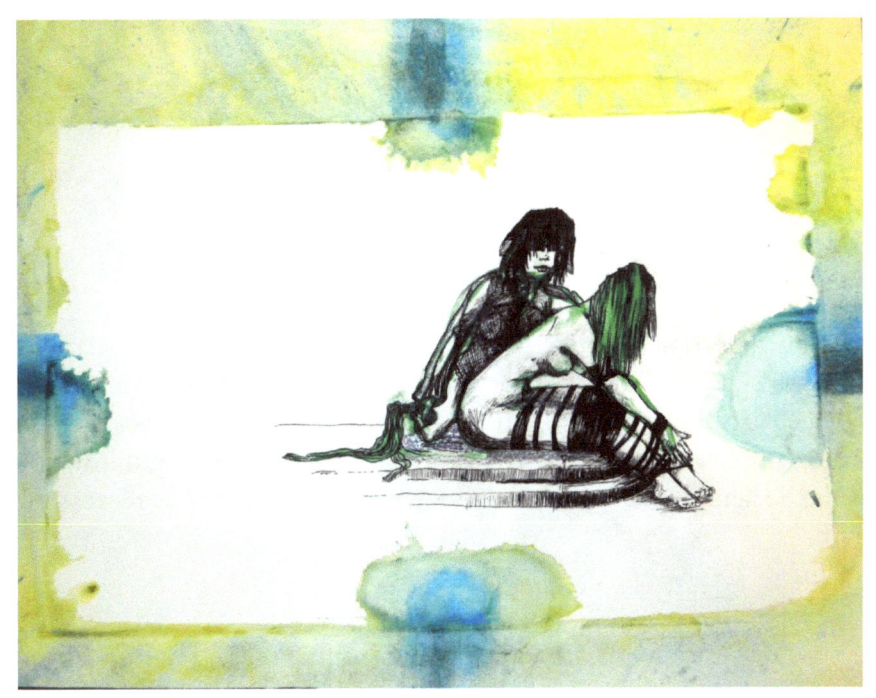

In the cold light of morning
Kimberly Walker
17" x 21"
WaterColour and Ink

Cold, isolated and lovely.

Lisolette Gilcrest

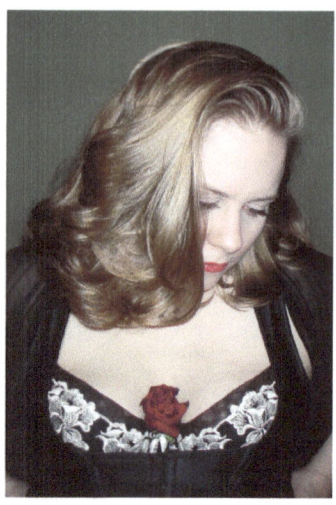

Featured in the permanent collection of the renowned Kinsey Institute's Special Art, Artifacts and Photography Collection, Lisolette Gilcrest is noted for her distinctly feminine and whimsical erotica that she says is focused less on "the deed" and more on the delicious intangibles. Lisolette is a two-time Erotic Signature Winner (2009 and 2010), has been featured by the Erotic Review, as well as published in four other books, and is the founder of the Society for Women in Erotic Art Today. Lisolette is represented by Streetwise Art.

http://www.lisolette.com/

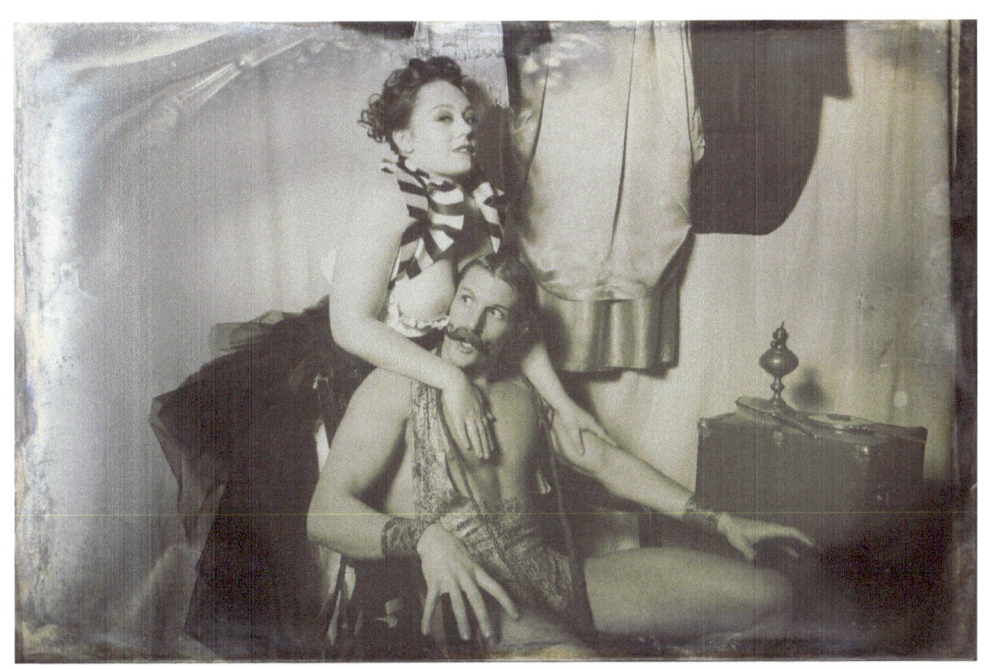

The Lion Tamer
Lisolette Gilcrest
18" x 14"
Digital Photography

Logan Miller

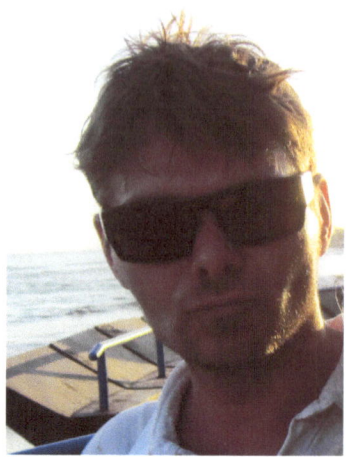

Logan loves speed and he loves his wood. He has been bending and carving lumber as long as he can remember. These days you'll find him in the shop, dancing to some old-school funk on his ipod, shaping raw wood into some of the finest boards in the world. He also enjoys snowboarding, girls and motorcycles, pretty much anything he can ride.

http://www.noblelongboards.ca

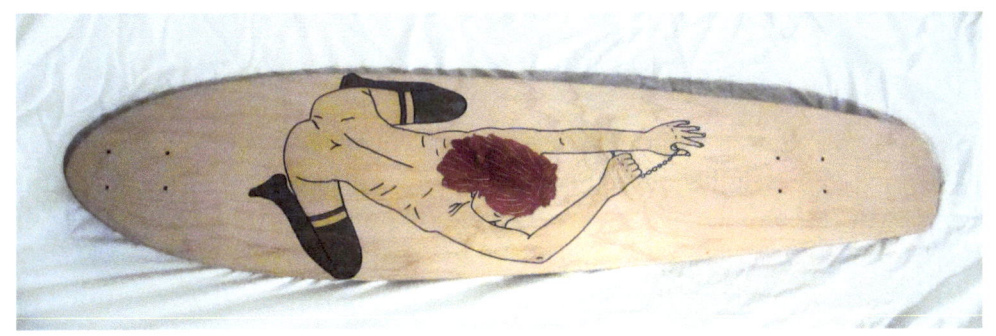

Waiting for Wood
Logan Miller
10" x 42"
Wood, Glue and Stain

The best ride.

Lynn Erin

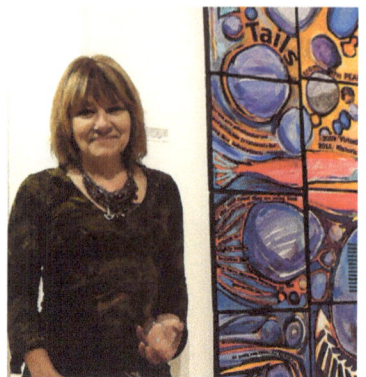

As a woman and a mother, Lynn has naturally honoured, and been challenged by the great Mother and the cyclical connection between herself, her child, her family, her work and the Earth. At 51, at this time in history, life as she knew it is changing…. She expects great new powers in this segment of her life. Knowing Lynn's independent, optimistic, activist spirit, one may be better able to see the sacred and silly that emanate from her heart and her art, both which often evoke emotion in a most primal way. Infused with a natural sense of humour, Lynn comes across at once contemplative, profound, magical and playful.

http://www.fireweedart.ca

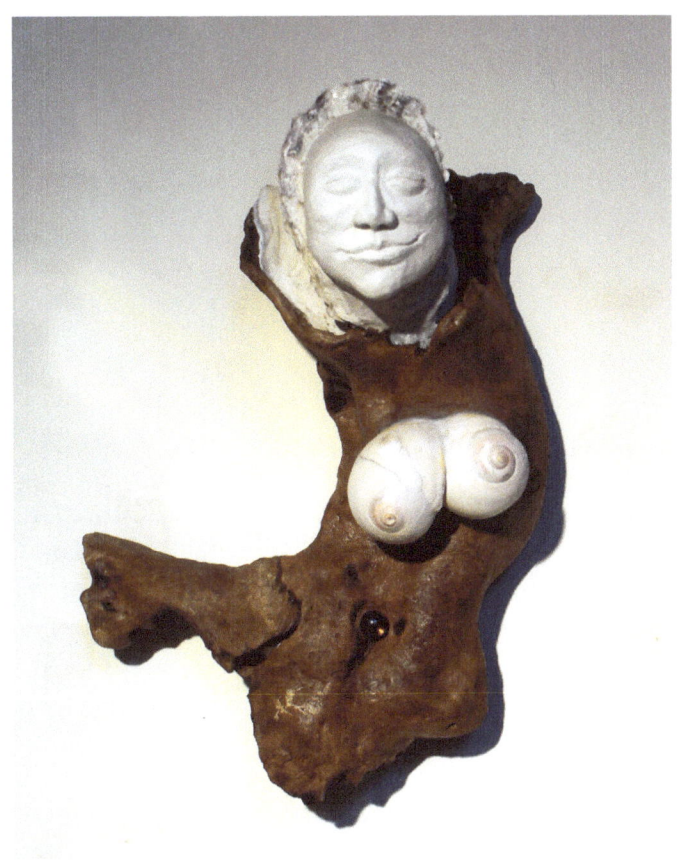

Moon Dance in the Oyster Bed
Lynn Erin
16" x 10" x 8.5"
Found objects and Plaster

These objects found me, in a Tide Pool,
Under a Full Moon and Wow,
How Erotic are Moon-Snail Shells?

Margot Stolz

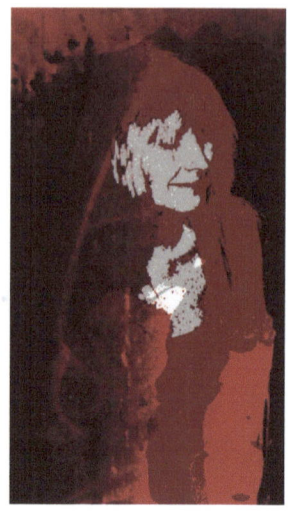

MARGOT is a South Okanagan based, mixed media and ceramic sculpture ARTist and invites the viewer to interact with her 3D works. MARGOT explores the "shadow self" (Jungian theory) inspiring her favourite themes: Archetypes & Erotica, The Sacred & Profane, Shapeshifter – Allegory of the ARTist's Psyche. A graduate of UVic/OUC in 1997 with a BFA and Diploma of Visual Arts in 1995, a B.Ed. in Art Ed. UBC 2005 and studied Art Therapy at the Kutenai Art Therapy Institute in 2010. MARGOT has exhibited her works in juried and non-juried Group and Solo Exhibitions extensively throughout the Okanagan. MARGOT is the owner of Studio 2012 in Summerland.

https://www.facebook.com/MargotStudio2012

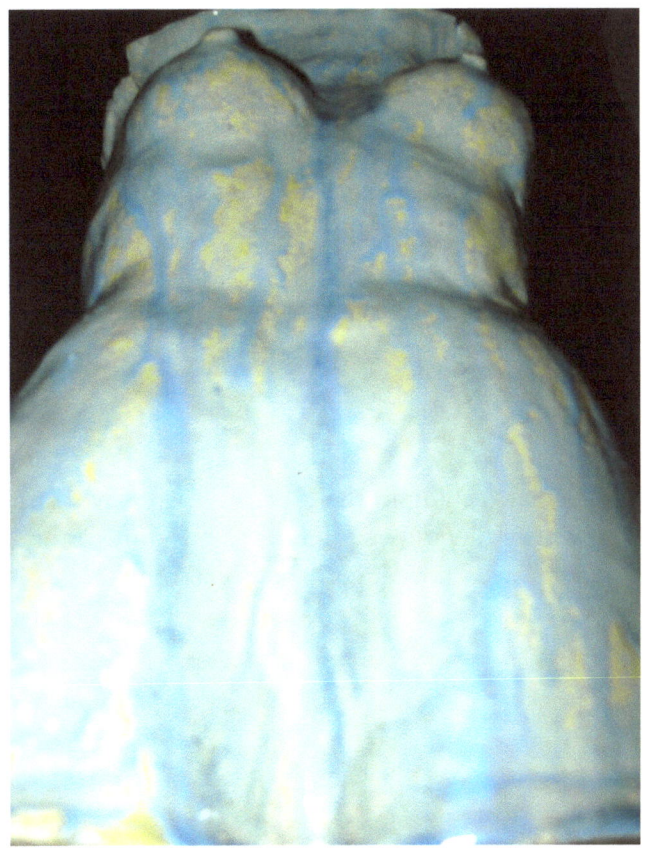

She's Wet
Margot Stolz
17" x 12"
Ceramic Sculpture

What does the thought of WET do for you?
Note: this is an interactive piece, the viewer will be invited to answer the question,
write it down and drop it into the sculpture (making an erotic wish)

Marianne Dashwood

Marianne is a self-taught writer currently living in the Okanagan area. Marianne has been drawn by her many lovers, most of whom were artists themselves. Her day job is quite traditional, and she has a secret life about which only a few select people have knowledge. You don't know her.

Or maybe you do.

Being Teased

I can hear his pencil on the paper, as I am lying completely naked
on the soft blankets, legs slightly spread, hips protruding, back arched.
I glance over under heavy lids. He licks his lips as he looks at me, and pauses.

I can sense his hunger as his pencil slides over my form, my folds, my belly, my breasts.
I know I glisten, I wonder if he can see. I inhale deeply, and my back curves upward
just a little,

I feel my nipples tickled by the air.

I wait for him.

It is tantalizing agony.

It feels like he is touching me lightly, barely perceptible, as he draws each part.
I imagine with each line drawn, I feel his kiss, his tongue.
I hear his breathing.
My back arches again, my knees spread a little farther apart.

He puts down his pencil.

Mario Vucinovic

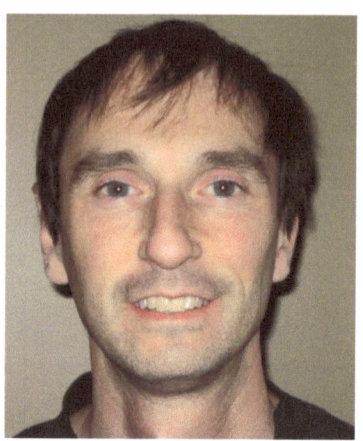

As husband and father of two, appreciatively calling Peachland, British Columbia home; a deserved recognition in that previous employment required travelling vast areas of this province: and transported at an early age years before, on the advice of family, when my parents emigrated from the former Yugoslavia and definitively chose to immigrate to Winnipeg, Manitoba and obtain Canadian citizenship. Typical barriers often associated with eastern European immigrants did not inhibit the pursuit of acquiring multi discipline degrees from the University of British Columbia in Education and Fine Arts; or an Electrical trade certification. Moreover, the ample studies of these barriers in terms of philosophical and psychological content have defined a large product of one self.

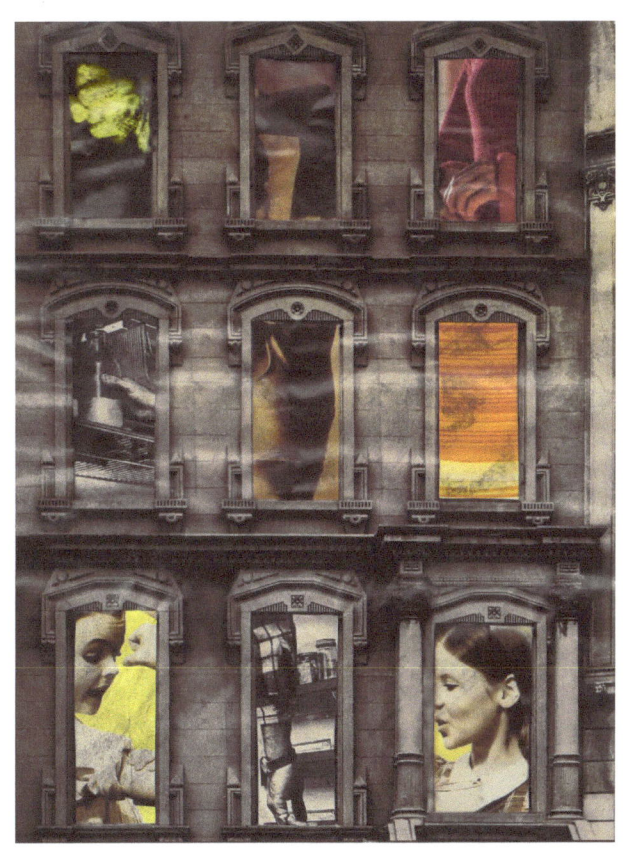

Milk and Honey
Mario Vucinovic
36" x 24"
Collage transfer to Digital print, Aluminum Mount

On a street there, when departing passing strangers' reflection of detachment
happens to become a spontaneous fetish of improvisation, luxuries await.

Martha Moore

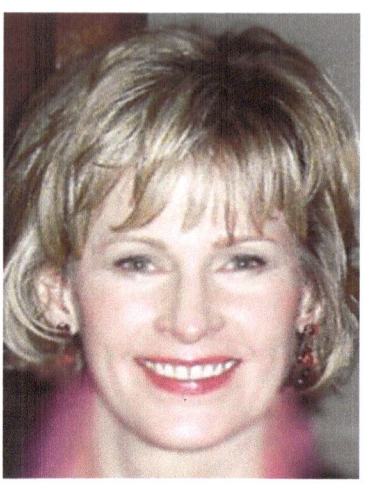

Martha Moore was born in Saskatchewan, lived for the past 30 years in Alberta and Ontario and has recently moved from Toronto to the beautiful Okanagan Valley to play more and work less. Martha has a BA Hon in Psychology and has spent her business career in corporate communications and the television broadcast industry. She is an active member of the Kelowna Art Gallery, Vernon Public Art Gallery, Lake Country Art Gallery and the Canadian Federation of Artists and her paintings have been exhibited in galleries and private collections in Toronto, Calgary and throughout the Okanagan Valley.

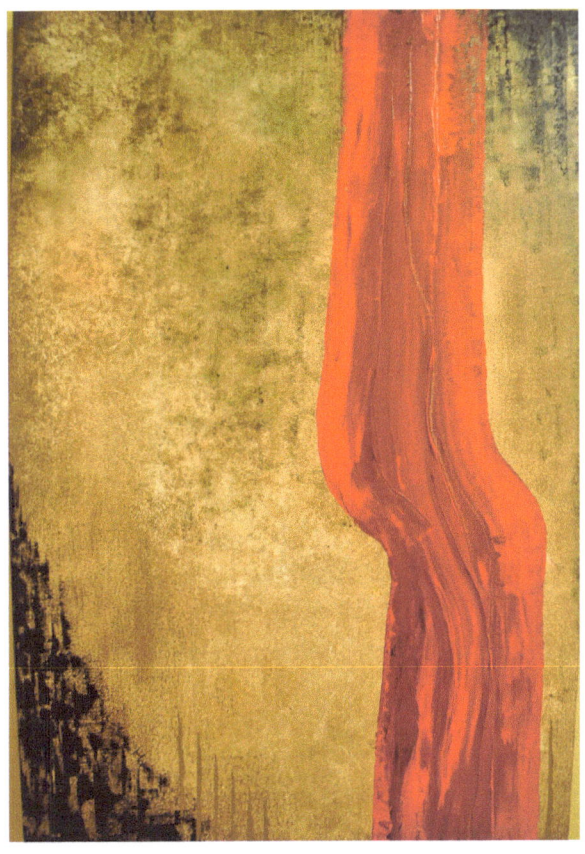

Fertility
Martha Moore
36" x 24"
Acrylic on Canvas

Through the heat of the union his seed is planted, it sprouts
and as her feminine body swells with child, so does his wanting and desire for her.

Mary Anne Domarchuk

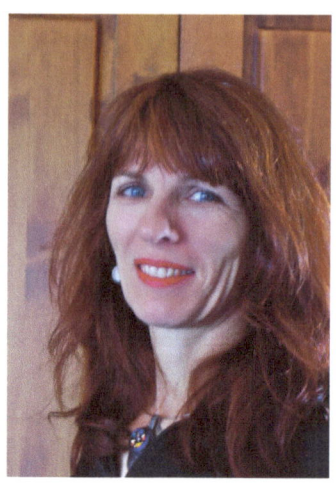

Mary Anne Domarchuk lives in Armstrong BC, a small but mightily artistic town in the north Okanagan. Mary Anne's interests in the human body are professional as well as recreational as she is the one and only public (misspelled, 'pubic') health nurse in Enderby, an even smaller but every bit as artsy town just north of Armstrong. She has three, young-adult children who regularly ask, 'Why can't you just be like other mothers?!" And, lucky girl, she has a sweetie who is well endowed with a cabin in the mountains where we pleasure in nature. He also enthusiastically supports her efforts to 'not be like other mothers'. Mary Anne hopes that as her children leave the nest she can spend more erotic time in both art and nature.

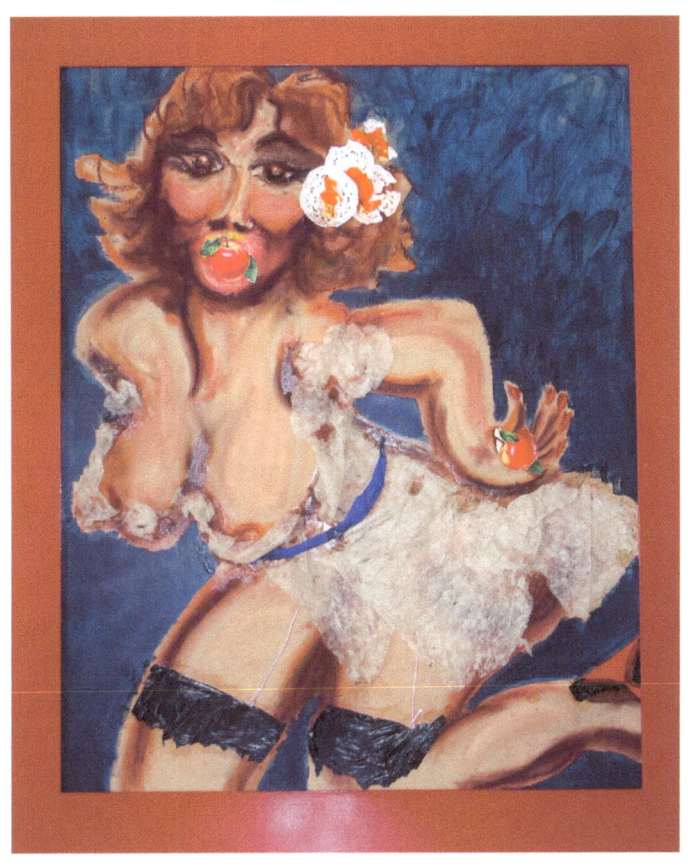

Apple Tart
Mary Anne Domarchuk
Mixed Media Drawing/Collage

What's sweet, juicy and a little flakey?....................A well put together 'Apple Tart'!

Michelle Stephenson

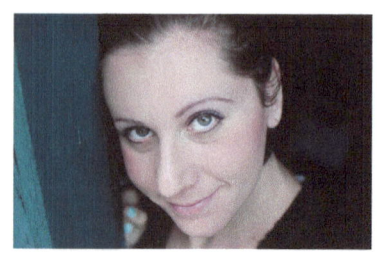

I believe in using the expressive form of photography to promote personal growth, and to aid as a stepping stool in my daily search for meaning. The Okanagan has been a rich source of inspiration, with the bright sun and cooling lake. Moving from Vancouver drew me out of a dark place, but I do like to go back and visit occasionally. I love to write poetry to accompany my photographs. I like to perform, and it scares the heck out of me. I am raising two young sons, passionately. I hope my sons grow up to respect strong women, and that they love themselves, and others, unconditionally. My husband is my rock, and I look forward to looking back at our life when we're 80. Our family is beautiful, and without them I couldn't achieve my dreams.

http://www.facebook.com/ContractPhotography

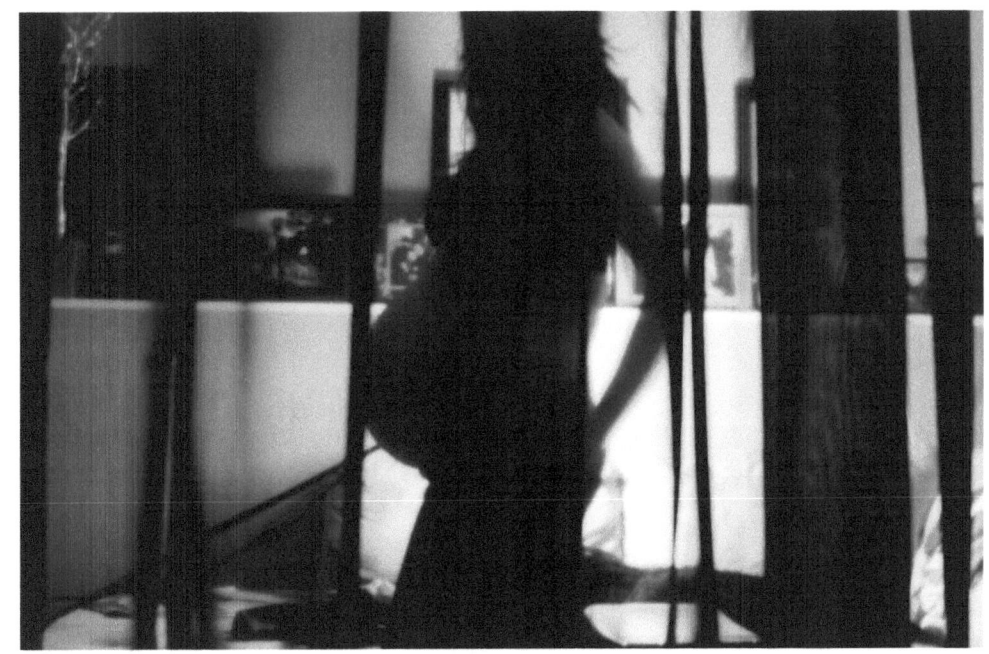

Undulation of Erotic Energy
Michelle Stephenson
12.5" x 18.5"
Black and White Photograph

The body sways with change.

Neal Campbell

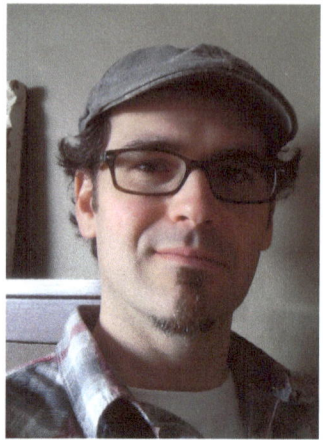

Neal is a recent import to Kelowna from Southwestern Ontario, where he was active in his local arts community. He is loving the Okanagan Valley and all it has to offer. Having come from somewhere relatively flat to this region of mountains and valleys has opened up his senses and fuelled his creativity. He is married with two teenage boys. He works in an office by day and when he has free time he likes to spend it drawing, photographing and drinking coffee – always while listening to music.

http://dortor.tumblr.com

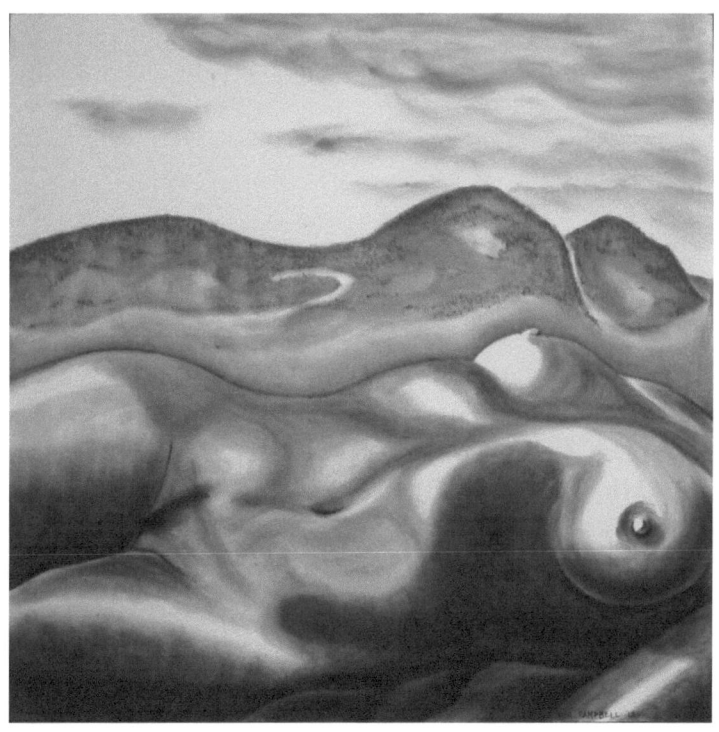

These Rolling Hills
Neal Campbell
24" x 24"
Charcoal on Masonite

There is mystery in the mountains…
they draw me in and make me want to explore every peak and valley.

Patricia Gulyas

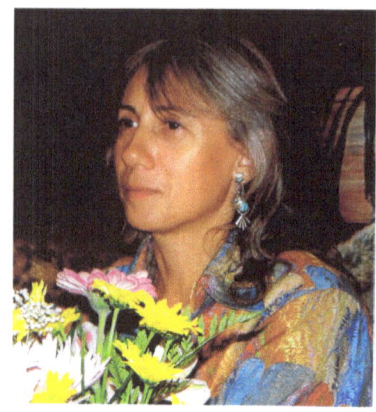

Bonjour! Polish dance and a Hungarian father who travelled through various countries for pleasure and work created Patricia's gypsy soul. Born and raised in France Patricia moved in Canada in 2001. Patricia studied fashion design, received her Window Dresser and Faux-Finish certification. Patricia is interested about many things such as the Hungarian and Japanese languages, Architecture and Art History. Animals are very important for Patricia and she found inspiration in Native Art and Philosophy. Moving in Canada required a career change and she began for a while truck driver and is a professional driving instructor part time. She crossed the country five times, three times from east to west in a car and twice from west to east behind an 18 wheel. Of course, one can't drive an 18 wheeler without listening to country music which is her favourite. But despite this, Patricia likes to create listening to blues. This may be why the blue color and the moon are present often in her painting.

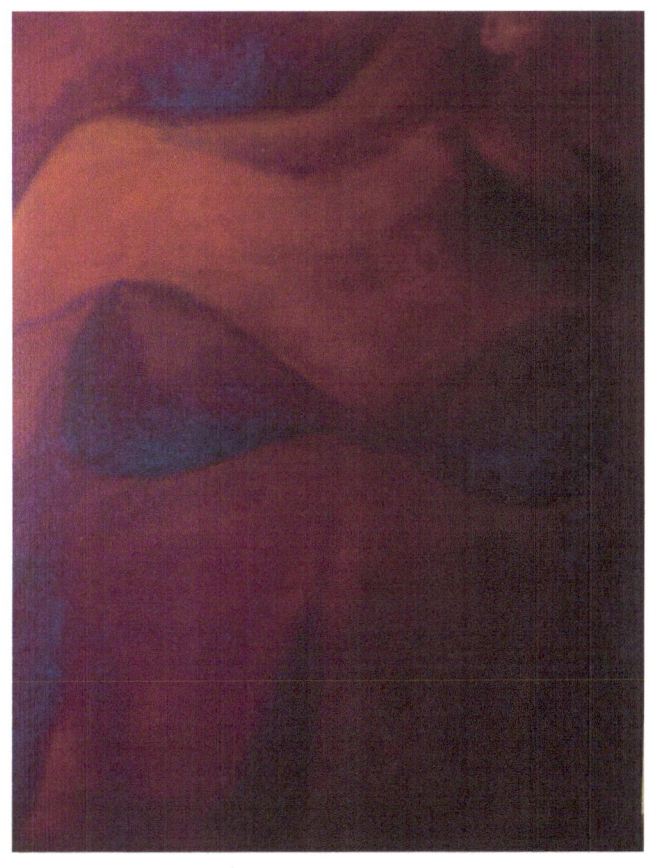

Dark Lady
Patricia Gulyas
24" x 18"
Acrylic on Canvas

''Warm wine lovely night.'
Hum! Some black grapes made some warm and deep red wine, almost blue!

Paul Butvila

Paul Butvila was born in England on November 24th 1953. He dabbled in Art as a child but began painting seriously at the age of 20, painting mostly in the style of realism, and was influenced by some of the modern day realists of our time. His studio is in Westbank BC.

http://www.butvilaillustrations.com

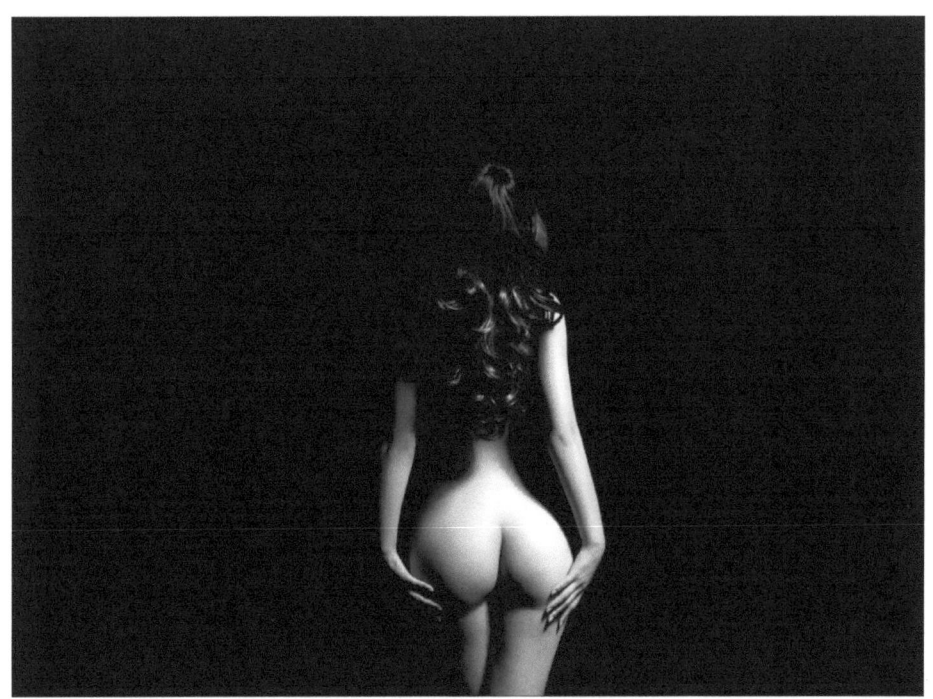

Dangerous Curves Ahead
Paul Butvila
20" x 16"
Acrylic on Board

You imagine the softness of her curves, the warmth of her skin
as you imagine what she has in store.

Randal Sweet

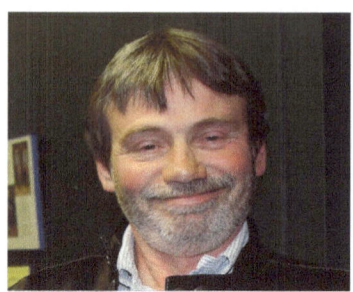

I've been a housepainter for 30 years. Now semi-retired I took up painting on canvas. I guess I just have to be painting something!

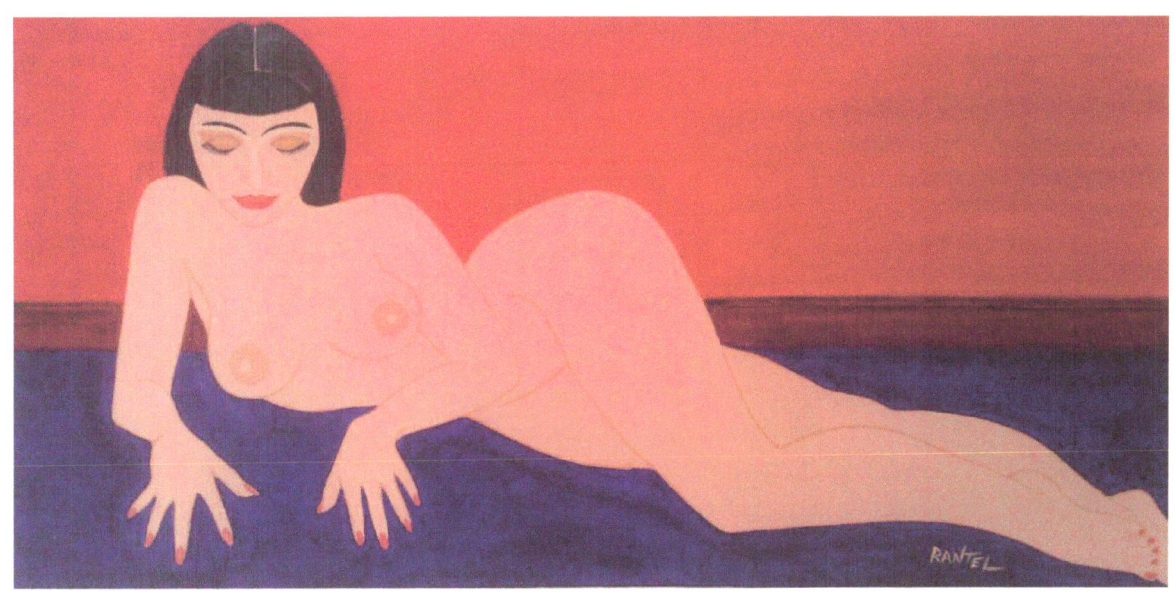

All Made Up But What to Wear?
Randal Sweet
20" x 40"
Acrylic on Canvas

Anticipation of an encounter can be the highpoint of the evening.

Rena Warren

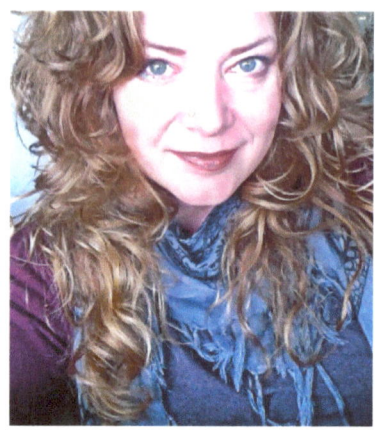

Rena Warren is an Okanagan based artist, art educator, world traveler and most importantly; a single mother. She moved to the Okanagan in 1991 to attend Okanagan University College where she received her Bachelor in Fine Arts. She worked on and off at Opus while raising her daughter and pursuing a post degree in education at the University of Victoria. Aside from her various teaching gigs over the years, Rena likes to spend her time traveling throughout India, cooking, gardening, blogging and creating art. In her private practice, Rena specializes in large-scale oil portraiture and original block print designs. Her extensive travels throughout India form a large part of her inspiration and subject matter.

http://www.capricornucopiaartworks.blogspot.com/

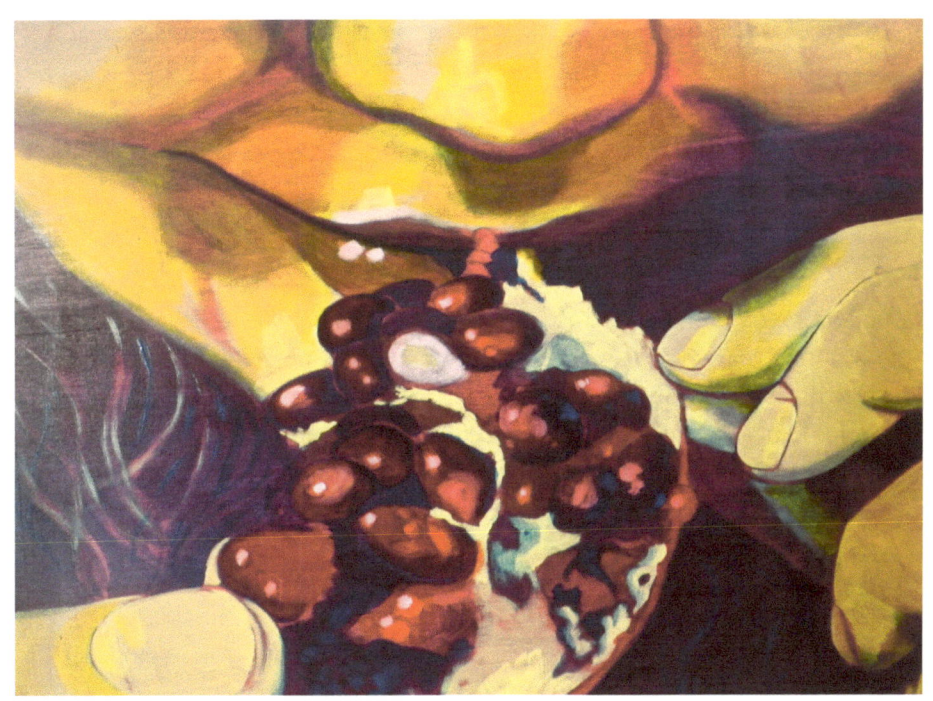

Pomegranate Eaters ~ "Eating"
Rena Warren
20" x 24"
Oil on Wood Panel

I have chosen to portray the consumption of pomegranates as a metaphor for stages of seduction.

River Lewis

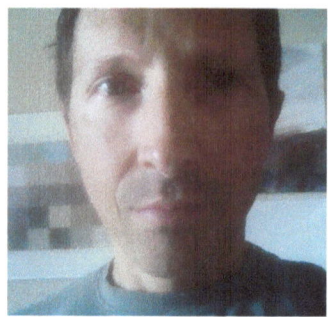

One of Lewis' first artistic memories is drawing at the Musee des Beaux Arts de /Montreal/ Museum of Fine Arts when he was five years old. It was a very intense time politically in the cities of Quebec - quite the opposite of a child's interest in things fine and beautiful. Previously the Managing Editor of Photography at BC Virtual and a virtual modeler, Lewis is the founder of Brew Gallery in downtown Vernon. He has curated exhibitions of digital art, drawing, painting, and photography. He holds a BFA in studio arts from Emily Carr Institute of Art and Design and teaches painting and drawing for the North Okanagan Arts Council.

http://www.riverlewis.com

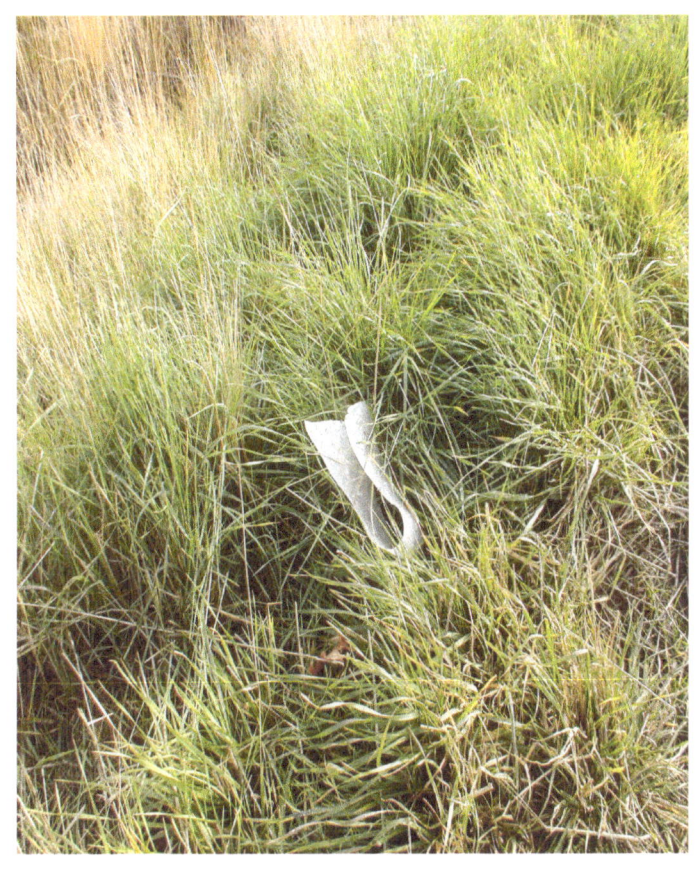

Polyan Au Naturel
River Lewis
20" x 16"
Digital Photo Print

She was laying asleep by the side of the road where the note said,
"WAKE ME UP IF YOU'RE GOING TO THE GALLERY. I DESERVE TO BE THERE."

Robert Verigin

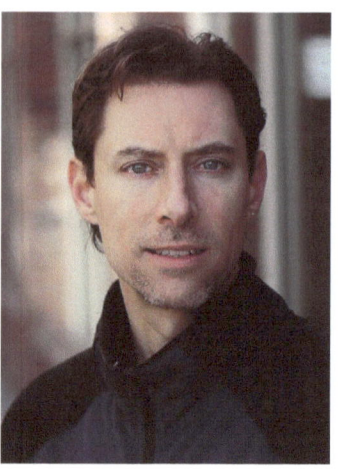

Robert Verigin has been a photographer for over 20 years. He was raised in the Kootenay region of British Columbia, Canada before moving to the Okanagan. Robert is skilled in many aspects of digital photography, has won numerous awards, and shows regularly at fine art galleries.

He currently lives in Kelowna B.C. where he works in the Art and Picture Framing industry and continues his photographic practices.

http://www.robertverigin.com

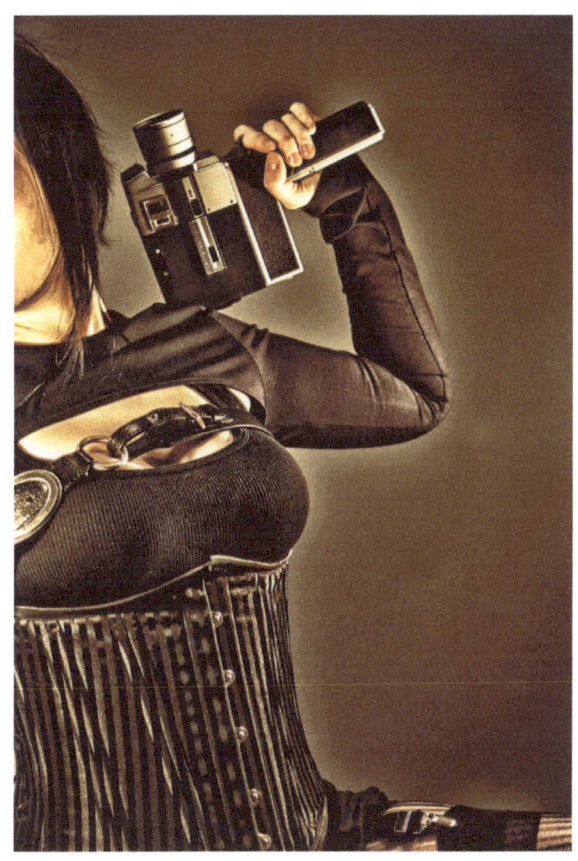

Take One
Robert Verigin
23" x 17"
Digital Photography

A private screening of leather and passion.

Robin McDonald

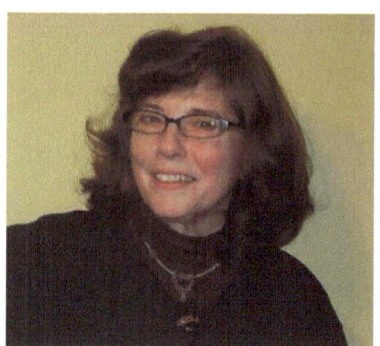

I have lived in the Vernon area for 10 years, transplanted from Vancouver. Since moving here I have been involved with the North Okanagan Artists Alternative, Powerhouse Theatre, the Vernon Art Gallery and currently work at the Vernon Community Art Centre. I have really enjoyed being involved in the rich artistic community in Vernon. We are blessed here to be surrounded by so much creativity. I have a nice dog who also loves art and artists as well. I am currently working on studio upgrades, and hope to be up and running again soon.

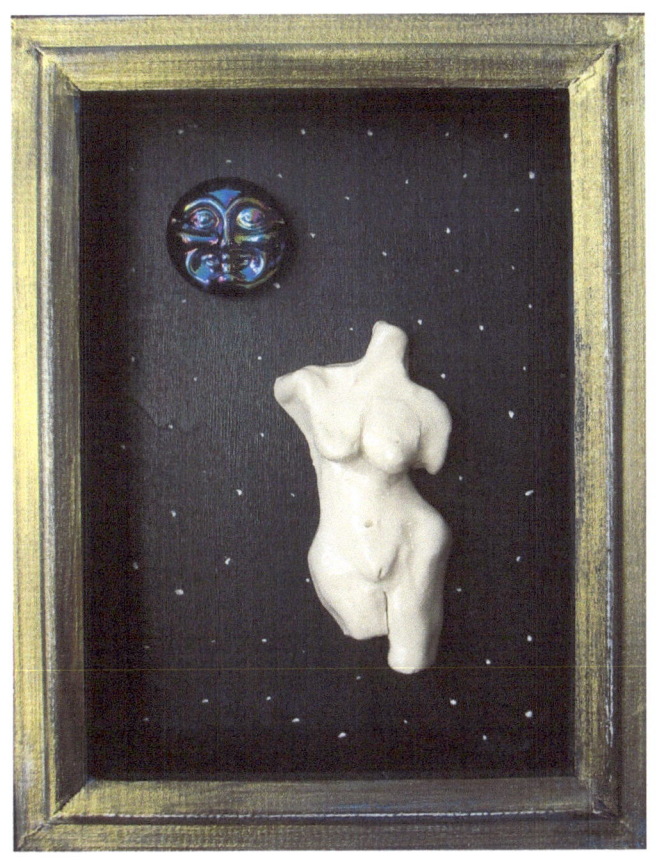

Venus and the Moon
Robin McDonald
6.5" x 8.5"
Mixed Media

Venus and the moon are always united in my mind.

Roxi Sim Hermsen

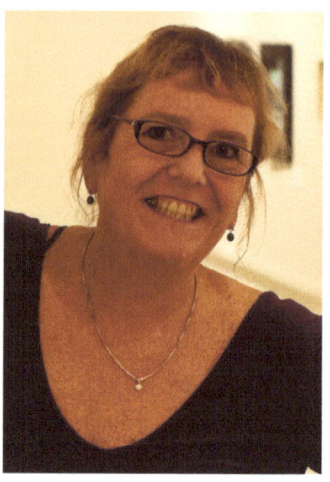

BEd FA Dip. FA 5th year counseling. Vernon based artist Roxi is a real "Culture Vulture," and Bohemian at heart. She loves to travel and be inspired by cultural dress, dance and music. Together with Tony her husband of 34 years she has led a creative life as a potter, sculptor, painter, tap dancer and teacher. Roxi started painting seriously in 1997 in Grenada W. I., going through 200 ft. of canvas and a suitcase full of paint. In 2004 she and Tony oversaw a relief effort sending a tonne of relief supplies and seeds to Grenada after the devastation of Hurricane Ivan.

Roxi is very community oriented helping to found the Salmon Arm Art Gallery, the Salmon Arm Folk music society, the Enderby and District Arts Council, the Okanagan Artisan's guild, the Enderby Wild Wallflower Community Mural Concept and, with her parents and Tony, The Okanagan Science Centre. Roxi is currently developing healing art workshops and webinars. Her first webinar on her Pearls of Wisdom Tarot workbook/journal will take place on Global Spiritual Studies April 1st. She is soon to be teaching Old School Tap at the Hub in Vernon.

http://www.RoxiArtWork.com

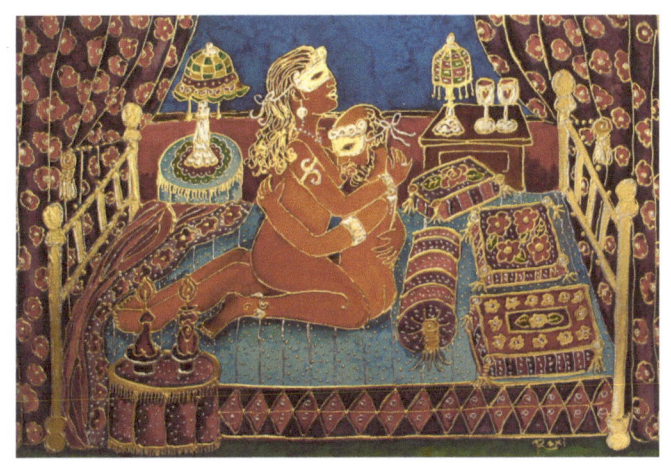

Titillation
Roxi Sim Hermsen
19.5" x 25"
Mixed Media

Simply "nipplelicious!"

Ryan Robson

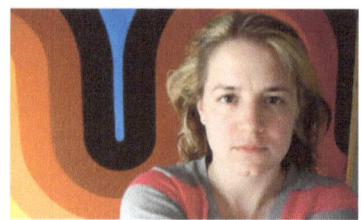

Ryan Robson was born and raised on Cape Breton Island and graduated from NSCAD University in 2009. She is a member and a huge supporter of THE HUB ARTS COLLECTIVE in Vernon. Every community needs a space to express and behave freely and THE HUB provides and encourages just that. With a belief in the power of art and the desire to challenge the representation of gender roles in popular culture, Ryan has come to the question, what is love and sex without gender? While she investigates this question she will continue to rub and touch and drip and lick and drool.

http://www.thehubartscollective.com

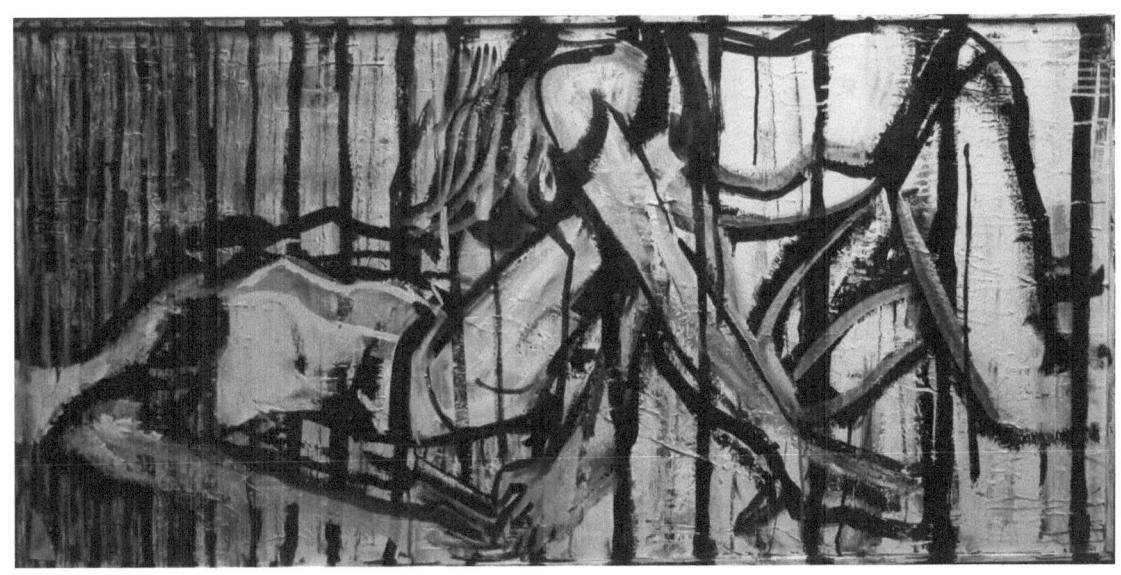

Love Beyond Gender
Ryan Robson
60" x 30"
Acrylic

What if there were no rules, what if there were no expectations,
would we allow each other to be each other.

Sandra Windsor

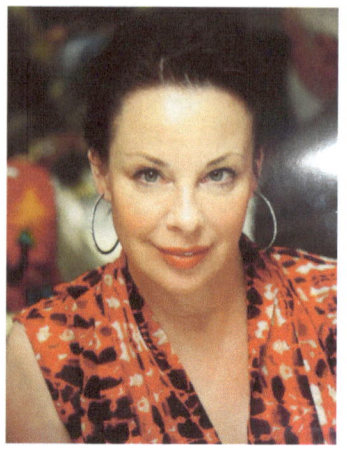

Sandra is originally from the coast ....Vancouver Island and the gulf islands area., growing up by the sea. She states I have salt in my blood....Sandra has been a resident of of Lake country in the Okanagan for the past eight years. She also said what a beautiful place to be...... She is involved in many different art forms...... Sandra or Sam she is called for short is an active artist model......continually drawing and painting.....and has recently gone back to dance in the last couple of years.....Flamenco, Ballet and Jazz..... Sandra said these disciplines seem to complement each other and keep her motivated one for the other. When she creates art, she usually tries to think of what others might find pleasurable or humours in her work....Her ideas come from many different avenues usually the arts and nature. Sandra hopes you enjoy her work serious or funny.

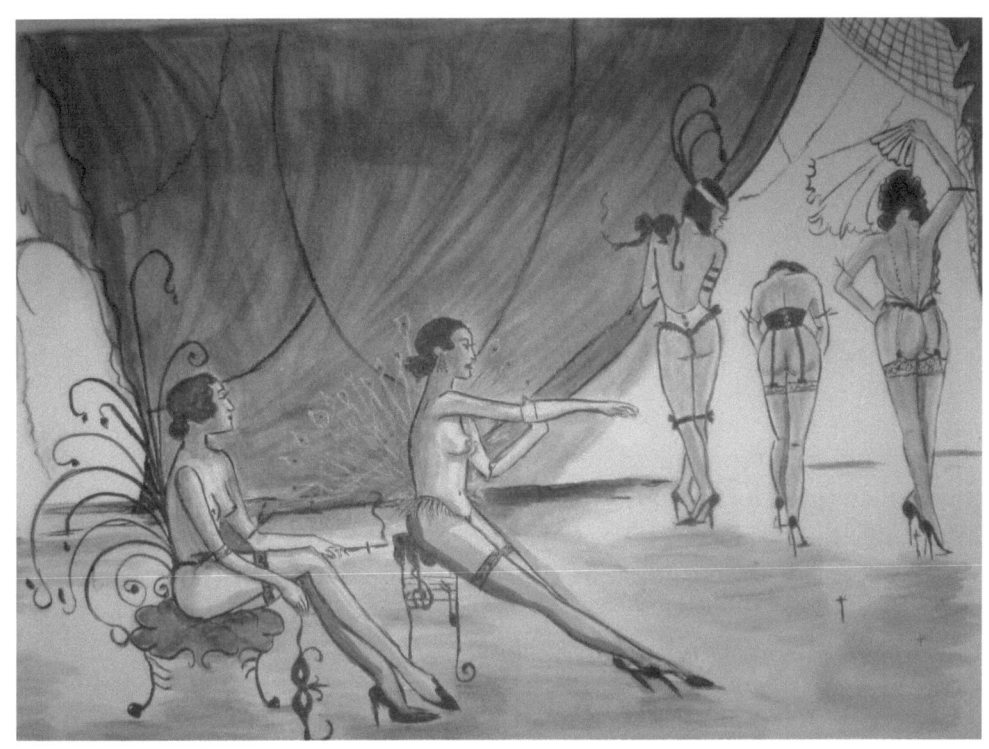

Backstage Burlesque
Sandra Windsor
22" x 28"
Mixed Media on Board

Gazes for details.....giggle of course.......it's all for the observer.......that which is you.

Sea Dean

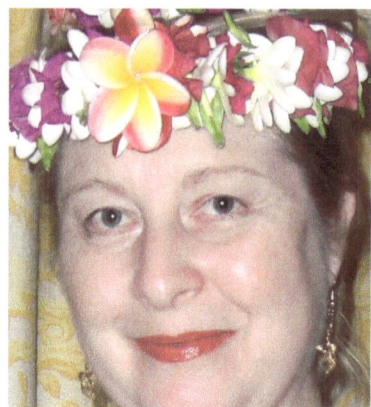

I became a professional Artist more than 30 years ago. I roamed the world and had so many wonderful experiences but somewhere I lost sight of what was important to me. The year 2,000 heralded major change and rekindled the determination to live my dreams. Now as an Artist and Art instructor, I rise each morning vibrating with excitement. It is so good to be alive.

http://www.facebook.com/BlueSkyRedEarthGallery
http://www.canvoo.com/artists/sea-dean

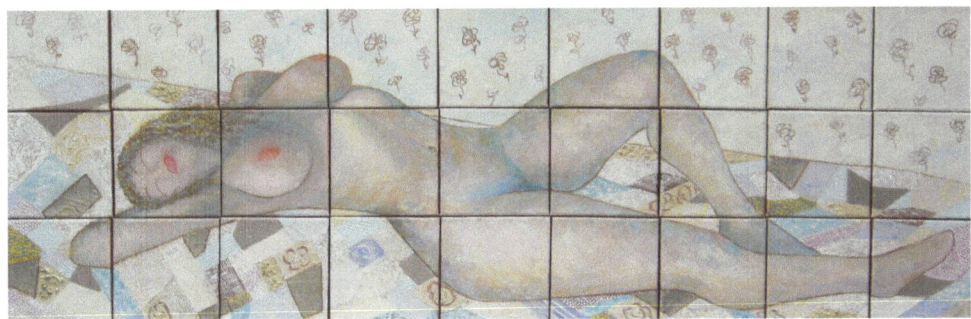

Camelia
Sea Dean
18" x 54"
Acrylic

You will never tire of Camelia; this "Puzzle Painting" has almost 3,000 variations.

Shannon Breadner

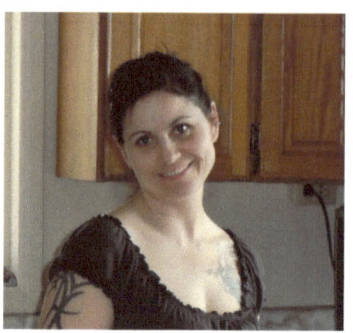

Not being a native Okanagan I grew up in many different places in Canada before settling in Kelowna. Being a free-spirited soul I gravitated to nature, spirit and eventually combining different beliefs and incorrporating it into my everyday being. Getting inspiration from this way usually comes from meditating, woman/ pagan groups and drumming circles. Woman have always been a beautiful subject for me ever since I was a child, combined with the spiritual and erotic nature they have evolved to what they are today.

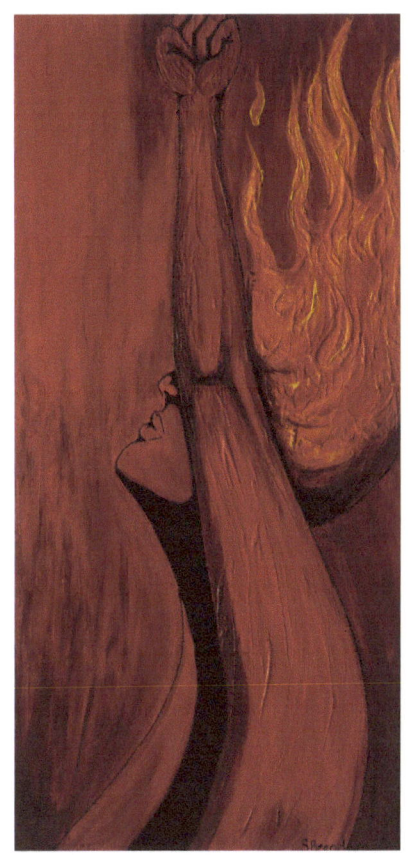

Fire
Shannon Breadner
16" x 9"
Acrylic on Canvas

By the fire of her bright spirit.

Sharr

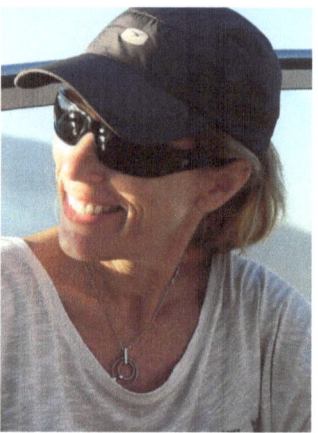

Sharr houses a treasure chest of memories, ideas and precious moments derived from her unique life experiences. A wanderer from birth, Sharr grew up on military bases posted around the world, finally settling as a young adult, in Canada, Although she calls Kelowna, BC her home, Sharr is a pilgrim at heart. A soulful traveller, Sharr has a gift for seeing the extra ordinary in the ordinary, living life with a passion and intention, which extends into her writing form. An interest in Eastern Philosophies, Buddhism, Tantra, Religious studies and cultres has migrated into a eclectic blend of knowledge, enabling Sharr to teach, mentor and write from a deep sense of sensuality, passion and penmanship.

Cherry Picking
by Sharr

Bunches of cherries hang from the trees
Nuggets of flesh, impregnated by bees.
Families of Foreigners flock to the fields
Selecting the ripest, the plumpest, the sweetest
That the orchard can yield.
Laughter and language mesh into one,
Reaching and picking till each tree is done.
I listen, I watch, I observe,
I feel.
Alone in the Orchard, Alone, and surreal.
But not like Salvador Dali,
who painted his fears.
More like a Sage,
who grew with the years.
Everywhere I look I see harvest and wealth
Families and cherries,
Abundant with health.
But here is a cracked one, the flesh raw and bared,
Left alone in the orchard frightened and scared.
Not to be picked, selected or chosen.
Never to be sliced, boiled or frozen.
How does a cherry feel?
Left on the branch.
Was it purposely ignored or missed just by chance?
I choose to believe, I choose to hope
That one lonely cherry has methods to cope.
With the feelings of loneliness, rejection and loss
Being the one with the stretch marks.
The one that got tossed.

The Surrender by Sharr

I think I met her online, or was it at an airport, juggling her bags as I perceived an aura of children dancing around her head? Or perhaps it was on an escalator, her slender frame ascending above mine? It doesn't matter any more; suffice to say, we met. And have continued to meet, as the years have unfolded, and the timeline grows fuzzy with a new generation of children conceived, educated and matured.

Destiny, encapsulated. A clumsy introduction, a shared desire, intentions stated, an agreement made. Let the dance begin. And so it was.

And here we are, once again, in another town, another place. Settled into a nondescript hotel room bearing no clues as to our geographical location. Wooden, stick furnishings line the wall, illuminated by dim lamps, supporting 40-watt bulbs providing just enough light to see, not enough to see well. Rectangular mirrors strategically hung for ease of dressing, minor costume adjustments or final lipstick applications as the businessperson begins their day.

But she is on top of me, and the mattress is deceptively soft - a cushion top affording an added degree of comfort, a decadent lushness in contrast to the sparseness of the room – which may or may not have been as described above. Her slow rhythmic movements taunting me, our eye's locked in a passionate embrace, I listen for the telltale short intake of her breath, as I penetrate deeply inside her, feeling the damp softness, every cell of my body awake, alive with desire, anticipation, knowing.

"May I help you?" I questioned, catching the falling bag, extending my hand in friendship to this exquisite woman. "Do you travel often?" Her response was immediate, open, friendly, relief as her burden was lightened. We walked away from the baggage carousel, towards the exit.

The same eyes reflected back at mine today, only softer, deeper, veiled with desire, concentration, anchored in the present moment. I pull her down towards me, wanting her body aligned with mine, unable to resist the temptation to take control, needing to feel her skin against my chest, her hair tickling my body, the warmth of moisture on my neck as I listen for her next exhalation, and I thrust deeper into her cavernous wetness.

She resists. I feel her legs tense around my hips, her arms push back against my chest, her lips part to reveal a slow smile of recognition. "Not yet," she whispers. I watch her tongue dampen her lips and crave for it to be in my mouth, sucking it deeply, heightening her sensations of arousal as she extends it, stretching outwards, towards me, towards mine.

Kali – my Tantric Goddess of darkness, fire, death. Dominating over Shiva in a waltz of destruction, enslavement, and salvation. Powerless to resist, I succumb to her desires. Feel my body relax into the dance of time, as her undulations increase, searching, seeking, deepening her hold, the union of the Yoni and the Lingam.

Mesmerized by her beauty, I watch her, feel her, taste her, listen to her low almost silent moans of passion, rising from deep within, a primal sound awakening my lust, my need to capture, control, devour, succumb. Biceps bulging I grasp her waist, holding her pelvis to mine, and once more our eyes meet, her hypnotic gaze penetrating deep into my soul, as I feel the burning fluid escape from her loins, bathing the bed in an ever widening pool of dampness, and she concedes, collapsing against me in a universal gesture of surrender.

"I want to learn." She had said. "When the student is ready, the teacher appears." I replied nonchalantly, in a vain attempt to hide my rising anxiety, my increasing desperation to know this woman intimately.

"But who will be the student?" she responded, a knowing smile lighting her eyes, as she raised her arm, and hailed a cab.

Suzanne LeStage

My essence is that of a country girl who grew up on a farm on Vancouver Island. This environment was tempered with an exposure to art of the masters with a trip to Europe's art museums at a young age. With a childhood surrounded with classical music and art history and hours spent dreaming in the country fields and in the forest, my works cannot help but reflect these influences. i have resided in the Okanagan with my husband and children for the past 12 years and travel extensively for privately commissioned works.

http://www.EyesofLeStage.com

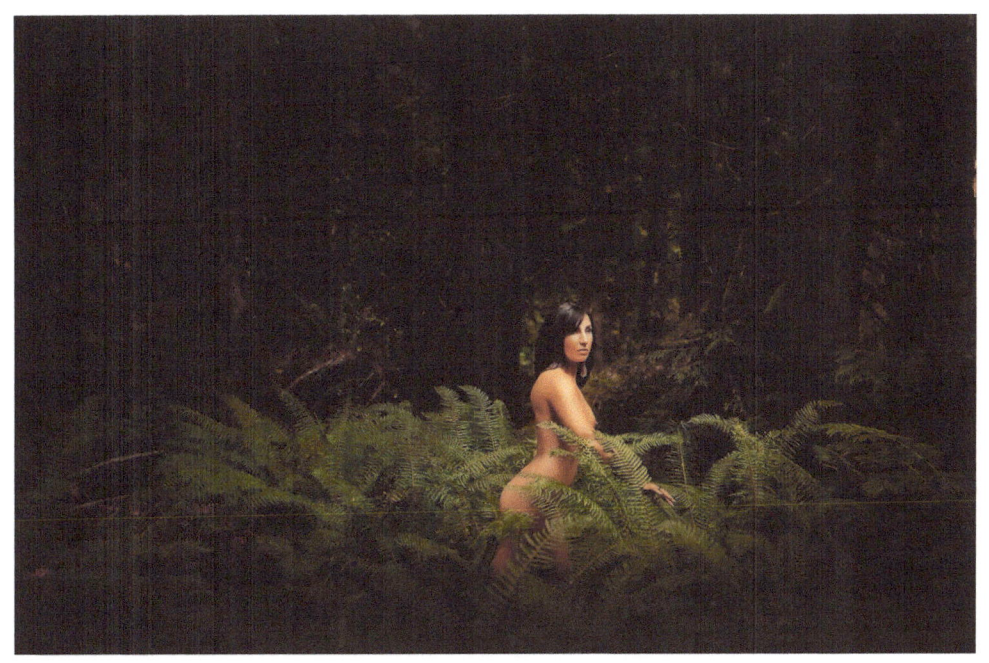

L'apres-midi d'un Faune I
Suzanne LeStage
20" x 30"
Photograph

Awoken in the forest by the sounds of a beautiful forest nymph
making her way through the bed of ferns.

Teri Blackwell

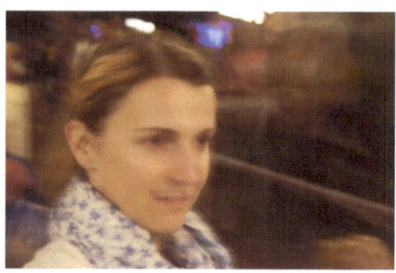

I am a wife, mother of three and an artist consecutively. My husband and I packed up our two children and moved to Kelowna nine years ago from Prince George looking for a change of scenery and if available to us, a little adventure. We soon increased our brood by one and settled in to our own home and the sunny Okanagan lifestyle we had anticipated. Besides drawing and painting some of my other passions include mountain and road cycling as well as yoga and pilates. My husband and I encourage a healthy active lifestyle in our children and anyone else who is willing to join in.

http://www.tlblackwell.com

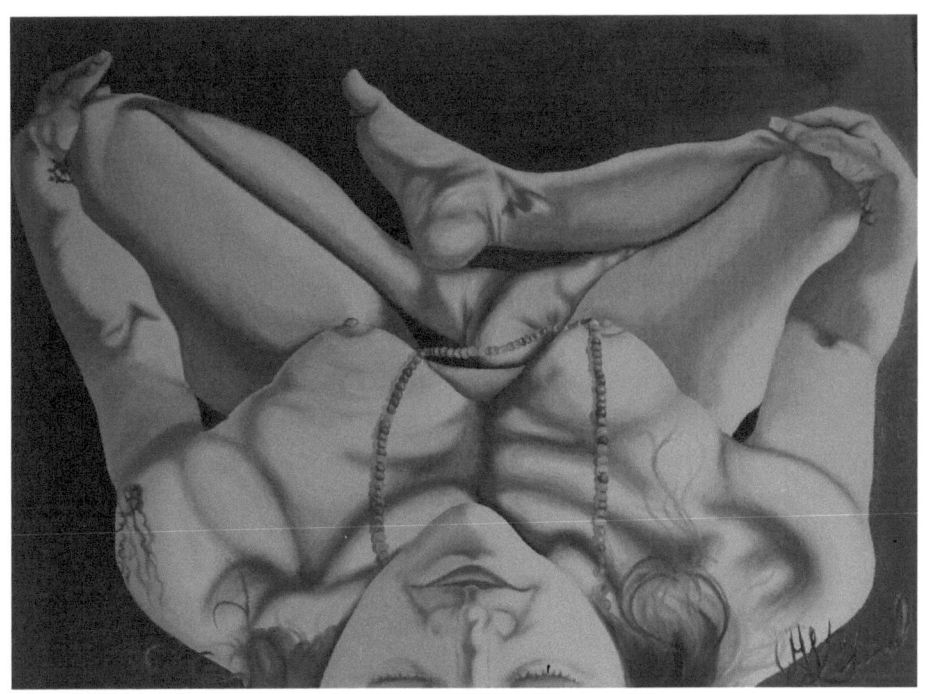

Lou
Teri Blackwell
18" x 24"
Oil on canvas

This portrait I created based on a photograph I took
at a sitting with my best friend Louise Stout.

Tina Aziz-Siddiqui

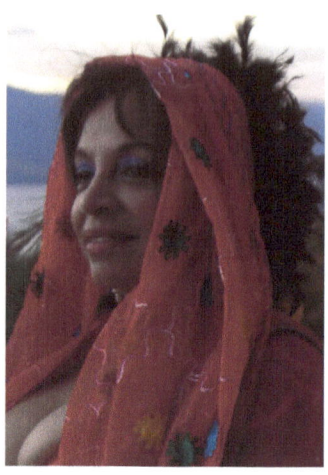

Born and raised in Pakistan, I travelled within the country and overseas with my diplomat father. Trained as a Graphic Designer, my artistic journey has been that of an explorer. Working in a variety of mediums, collage and mixed media top the list for me at the moment. I find Life drawing very thrilling, hence the figurative works were done in sessions with models. Often enjoying an "explosion" of colours, I find working with a limited palette equally thrilling. Light cascading over forms, is the driving force that compels me to paint as I strives to capture a specific moment in time. Portraits, and landscapes are the other themes I am currently painting.

Since 1976 I have exhibited in group and solo shows in United Kingdom, USA, Canada, Pakistan and Dubai. In 2004 I moved to Kelowna after a 13 year stay in Dubai.

http://creativepassion-tina.blogspot.com/
http://fineartamerica.com/profiles/tina-siddiqui.html

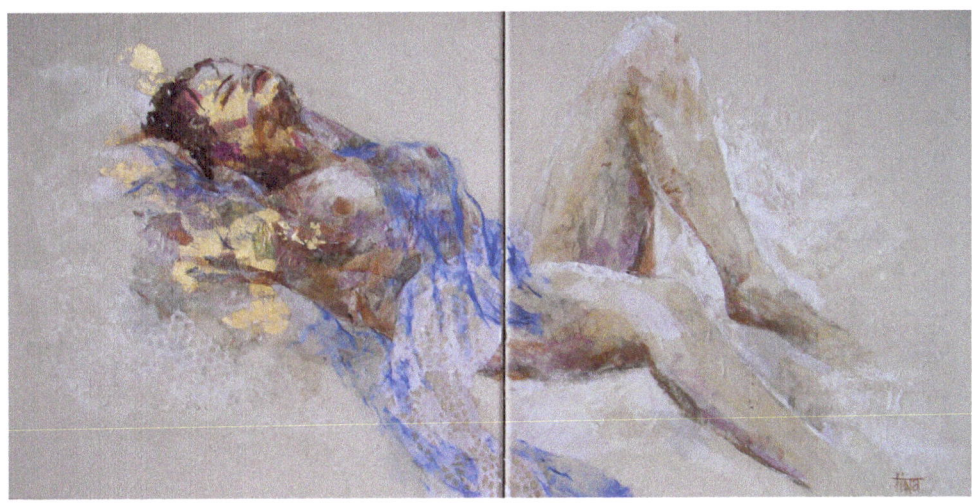

Breakfast in Bed
Tina Aziz-Siddiqui
16" x 32"
Collage on Canvas

All senses are aroused upon waking up, humbled by her hunger ....
she longs for the touch and much more, of a benevolent, cooperating participant.

Wendy Pros

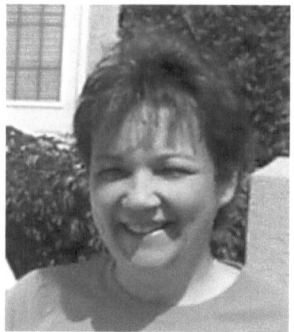

Born and raised in the Okanagan, and which I still reside. I am a self-taught artist, beginning with pencil I later went to charcoal and now my favorite medium…… scratchboard.   I am a professional dog groomer by trade during the day and a scratch artist by night. Being somewhat of a perfectionist, I am addicted to detail, and find that my addiction can be fed by the details nature has to offer, be it in wildlife the human form or the sleek lines of a classic car.

http://www.scratchinimagesstudio.weebly.com

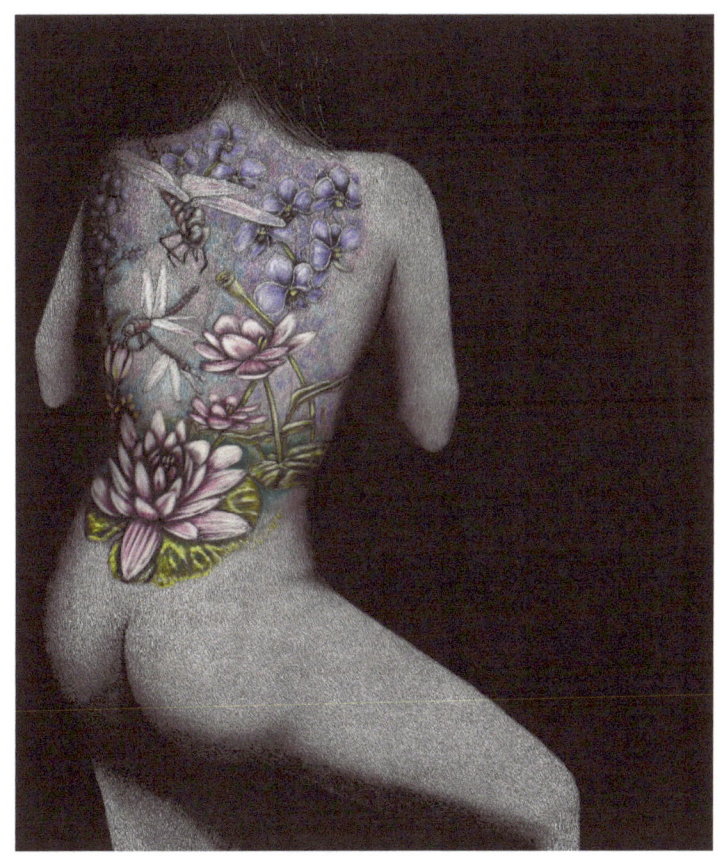

My Back Garden
Wendy Pros
20" x 16"
Scratchboard

Soft to the touch, yet holds the aroma of hidden desires.

My heartfelt gratitude....

goes out to all the artists who participated in this year's show, whether or not they have work selected for display. I believe in you, all of you, and acknowledge and substantiate your importance in creating a sensual, erotic world for us to live in.

I do make a huge effort to acknowledge artists who participate in my shows. One way I do that is by the web site, another way is by the catalog. This catalog is my way of saying thank you. Catalogs give substantiation and solidity to an artist's work by saying it is important enough to be printed. I have the skills, and the knowledge, so why not... ?

For everyone, I hope you enjoy the work presented, and think about the concepts each of the artists are bringing to the table. Sensuality is a huge part of our world, and it surrounds us in every creative endeavour or facet.

See you all next year, maybe.

Rumour has it ..... (shhhh)

Julia Trops

http://www.okanaganeroticartshow.com
http://www.facebook.com/EroticArtShow
http://www.exnihilovineyards.com
http://www.facebook.com/ExNihiloWine

Notes:

www.ingramcontent.com/pod-product-compliance
Lightning Source LLC
Chambersburg PA
CBHW050715180526
45159CB00003B/1030